EFFECTIVE TRAINING

Gerardo Soto

Effective Training
Gerardo Soto

© 2022 Gerardo Soto Ostos

All rights reserved

The copyright of this work is the exclusive property of the author. Its total or partial reproduction, as well as the incorporation into a computer system or by any means (electronic, mechanical, photocopying or others), the copy or distribution either for commercial or non-profit purposes is prohibited.

Review and editing: Marjorie Daphnis and Gerardo Soto

Design: Roxana Soto and Gerardo Soto

Spanish to Engish Translation: Gerardo Soto

First edition, September 2022
gsotoo@solderh.com
www.solderh.com

INDEX

PROLOGUE — 9

CHAPTER 1
Story "From the Microphone to the Classroom" — 13

CHAPTER 2
Training Basics — 27
1. Training Elements — 28
2. Goal Setting — 29
3. Collection of Information — 30
4. Training Needs Diagnosis — 34
5. Technical Training Proposal — 36
6. Activities that are Done Before a Course — 38

CHAPTER 3
Story "From the Summit to the Precipice" — 41

CHAPTER 4
Planning a Course — 51
1. Schedule Activities — 52
2. Training Manual — 54
3. Course Presentation — 57
4. Materials Checklist — 61
5. Call Invitation — 63

CHAPTER 5
Story "My Passage Through the Financial Environment"   67

CHAPTER 6
Learning   79
1. The Teaching and Learning Process   80
2. Participant Learning   81
3. Accelerated Learning Techniques   85

CHAPTER 7
Story "Consultancy and Sports"   93

CHAPTER 8
Instructor Teaching   105
1. Instructor Skills   106
2. Teaching Techniques   112

CHAPTER 9
Story "A New Beginning"   121

CHAPTER 10
Post-Course Actions   129
1. Attendance List   130
2. Course Evaluation   132
3. Training Report   135

INDEX

CHAPTER 11
Story "Development and Growth" — 139

CHAPTER 12
The Protagonists of the Training Process — 149
    1. The Training Process in a Company — 150
    2. The Training Process in a Consultancy — 157

CHAPTER 13
Story "Evolving into a New Future" — 167

CHAPTER 14
E-Learning — 175
    1. History — 176
    2. Benefits — 178
    3. Limitations — 180
    4. In Company Online Courses — 181
    5. Open Online Courses — 185
    6. Design and Teaching — 186

CONCLUSIONS — 193

ACKNOWLEDGEMENTS — 197

BIBLIOGRAPHY — 199

EFFECTIVE TRAINING

PROLOGUE

There is an old joke among consultants in Organizational Development about the importance of training and in turn the devalued position that can have as a fundamental part of the growth of a company; they say that the CEO of a company talked to the CFO about the budget allocated for the training of its people during the year, to which the CFO exclaimed with great regret "why spend so much money on this", imagine that we trained them and then they decide to leave the company", to which the CEO sarcastically replies "even worse, imagine that we didn't train them and they decide to stay." This old joke is nothing more than the clear and punctual reflection of a myopic and limited culture, which sees training as an employer obligation to fulfill before the Ministry of Labor and Social Welfare, when in fact it should be seen as a medium and long-term strategy for the economic and operational growth of the same company.

Fortunately there are many people who see in Human Capital, the strength of the same organization and continuously seek their training and job development as an investment, the way to increase its human capital and therefore its power as a company. For these people it is a win-win agreement and that is why training should not be taken lightly, it requires a well-thought-out strategy and extremely specific objectives about what needs to be achieved.

In the last five decades, the concept of training has changed a lot; education systems have had to adapt to social demands that were not even foreseeable a few years ago. Particularly, in the course of the last two decades, a series of approaches have been imposed in the world of training to give options to the demand for education within companies; such as: diplomas, specializations, master's degrees, courses, among others.

Nowadays companies need highly qualified and trained personnel, not only in technical and operational matters, but in skills of an interpersonal, executive and even emotional nature. Many of these skills, controversially called soft skills, become fundamental in the decision-making and development of organizations themselves. For this same reason, the role of instructors and trainers becomes more relevant to be able to develop and execute courses and workshops that capture the interest of the participants and above all, that are

PRÓLOGO

applicable to the daily situations and challenges they face in their work career.

In this book the author proposes knowledge integration strategies that modify the processes and practices of teaching and learning. It becomes a detailed manual of the process of selling, developing, implementing and monitoring training within companies. In it, you will find in detail examples of transformation processes in the operation, organization and management of traditional and distance training.

The present problems and critical points that it is necessary to identify and analyze in order to design strategies that make it possible to improve the quality of this educational offer. All this from academic theory, but above all from the experience and experiences of more than two decades of the same author in the world of training and consulting.

This book was divided into two parts. The nones chapters are narratives and stories of his entire career, his experiences, satisfactions, sufferings, problems, learning, reflections, and changes. The even chapters adequately explain how to work to teach a course; what is done to be approved, the whole planning process, the teaching and what is reported after a course has been given.

EFFECTIVE TRAINING

Gerardo shares in this book in great detail his joys and disappointments, his teachings and misadventures; as well as the personal and professional relationships that have made him the successful consultant and instructor he is today and in which he shares this material with us.

Joselo Arizaleta
Master in Organizational Development and
Consultant in Labor Exploitation

CHAPTER 1
STORY
"FROM THE MICROPHONE TO THE CLASSROOM"

I never thought that I would have been dedicated to training for more than 20 years, moreover, I didn't even think that I would dedicate myself to it and less that I would have ease to exercise it.

When I was 14 I decided what I wanted to be in life, to be a sportscaster. Since I was a child I was always a sports fan. First I played soccer, then tennis, baseball, tae kwon do and then basketball.

Since I was a kid I loved watching sporting events on TV, especially soccer, baseball and tennis. I paid a lot of attention and I kept phrases from the sports narratives and then, when I played with my friends and my cousins, I liked to narrate what I was playing. So in high school I decided what I wanted to do in life was to dedicate my life to sports storytelling.

I researched and realized that there was no professional career or bachelor's degree as a commentator, the closest thing to this was to study the Bachelor of Communication Sciences.

That is how in January 1993 I entered the university at the Tec de

EFFECTIVE TRAINING

Monterrey. I was fortunate to be able to choose the career I wanted to study and at the university I thought was the best for me.

The career was not so difficult to pursue, but to finish it, the economic situation of my family was not the best. Halfway through my degree I was able to get a scholarship and had to work on weekends as a waiter in the party room of a friend's dad in order to raise money for my expenses.

In May 1997 I graduated with a degree in Communication Sciences. With the race I had very good basics, but I needed more to be able to become a sports commentator.

During that time I went to a couple of interviews with Televisa and TV Azteca, but in both, my dream was truncated because when I was castings and tests, I always got nervous. In addition, to be a commentator it is not only necessary that you like sports and know a lot about the subject, it is also very important to know how to speak well, without fillers, to be descriptive, empathetic and natural when speaking when you are being recorded.

So after my two stumbles I learned from a friend of my dad's that there was a specialized school for sportscasters, in fact, the only one in the country in 1998. That's how I entered to study my specialty of Sports Commentator at the Raúl de Campo Jr. Training Center.

FROM DE MICROPHONE TO THE CLASSROOM

In this school I had the pleasure of meeting my first two teachers, from whom I learned a lot. I am referring to Lauro Alvarado and Jorge "Che" Ventura (RIP). In the school of commentators I studied for two years. Each sports subject lasted three months and we always saw three themes: History, Regulations and Narration. I remember taking subjects such as: Football, Baseball, American Football, Tennis, Basketball, Martial Arts, Bullfighting and Athletics.

In 1999 the students were told that a new radio program had been opened in Grupo Acir, in which we could record sports capsules from three to five minutes, and if it had good quality, they could go on the air. That's how I debuted with a recorded capsule, which I called "Face to Face", and in which I compared two athletes of the same discipline. Every weekend they started spending my capsules on the radio show for a period of six months, until an opportunity that I did not expect appeared: on November 2, 1999 they broadcast my capsule in which I compared the former mexican race pilots, Adrián Fernández and Michel Jourdain Jr. That night I went out to dinner with my cousin Octavio and his girlfriend. Te restaurant in which we went to dinner, broadcast the race, surprisingly, Adrián Fernández won the race in Motegi (Japan) and the next day, it became the most important news of the day. There was no one on the show who knew about motorsport and as I had made the capsule they called me and told me on Sunday morning that I was starting live.

EFFECTIVE TRAINING

On November 3 at noon I debuted on the radio and fortunately, I was able to overcome the nerves, the intervention liked the producer and the "Che", who was the main host of the program. That's how I earned a space every weekend. My career as a commentator was starting to go up.

Radio is a very nice medium to work with, but very poorly paid. The work to do was on weekends because that's when there were more sporting events. That was why I had to look for a formal job in an office to be able to collaborate with the expenses at my parents' house.

In January 2000 I went to an interview with Barter, a small company that organized commercial exchanges, which was led by two young and brilliant entrepreneurs, Enrique and Alicia Enciso. The vacancy job was for a sales position. In addition to the interview they applicated me a skill test, in which I was awfull and did not sell anything, but they told me that they had seen me other skills, so they asked me if I was interested in the vacancy of Training Assistant. Despite having no experience, I accepted the proposal. That's how my life was full of work, in training from Monday to Friday, and on weekends as a sports commentator.

In March 2000 I had several differences with the producer and despite from my good relationship with Ché, I decided to leave the program and focus on my work at Barter.

Barter was a company that was initially small, with less than 30 people on the payroll, but with many things in common: mostly young people, under 35 years old, graduates of private universities, middle and upper class. The company's goals were demanding, but the work environment was very pleasant, very similar to continuing in college.

In my beginnings as an assistant I reported to Ricardo Sainz, the Training Instructor. He and myself, along with Jacqueline Flores (Recruitment) made up the Human Resources area. There was a lot of work to be done in my area and the first thing I had to do was to learn, learn and learn. The method of trading was not easy to assimilate and the system where customer information was captured was also difficult to understand. In Barter I realized that a great defect, can be a great quality. I had a hard time learning fast and that is a great virtue if you work in training, because then you have to design a content and explain it in a simpler way so that everyone can understand it. Ricardo was demanding of me as a boss, but he encouraged me to work, create content and learn; I started to like that.

EFFECTIVE TRAINING

Within a few months of my entry I was already mastering the Induction process, which was long and tedious for any new young person who entered the company. Barter began to grow in revenue and so did his organizational chart. Ricardo first gave me the opportunity to participate in some stages of the tedious Induction process; but my first full course as an instructor was when Bárbara Chaparro enter de company. She was the new Human Resources Manager and would be Ricardo and Jacqueline's direct boss. Barbara had to suffer my inexperience as an instructor, I was very intolerant and demanding, but at the same time I was very proactive and with a lot of gumption.

After a few weeks Barter hired another person in Recruitment because the company needed to hire and train a lot of people. Barbara enrolled me in an external course of "Competency-Based Interview Techniques", which helped me develop my skills of observation, empathy, patience and listening, keys in handling a good instructor. In that course I met Adalberto Samaia, an experienced and talented consultant, who was actually my first teacher in the field of training.

A few weeks later Barbara enrolled Ricardo and me in the "Training of Instructors" course, also taught by Adalberto, which helped me understand how to develop a course and what are the different ways of learning in people.

FROM DE MICROPHONE TO THE CLASSROOM

A few weeks later, Barbara hired Adalberto to redesign the Induction Course. She commissioned me to accompany Adalberto in the process, which must have been a nightmare for him. Back then, I was an inexperienced, demanding young man and I criticized inconsequential things. But that process helped me develop my creativity and realize that training doesn't necessarily have to be tedious, it can be fun. In the end, the work together led to the design of a new fun course and above all, reduced the Induction process from four to just one week; that saved the company costs and generated more productivity. As a result I had my first promotion and became an instructor. Ricardo would no longer be my boss and I would now report directly to Barbara.

By then, Barter was still growing and a merger was arranged with the American company BarterTrust, whose headquarters were in San Francisco, California.

By August 2000 there was a call on television for a talent contest organized by Televisa, the "Voices Draft" and in which the winner of that contest would attend the Olympic Games in Sydney. I was very happy at Barter, but I had the "a restlessness" within me of the vocation as a commentator. At first I didn't want to participate in the contest because I was sure I wasn't going to win.

EFFECTIVE TRAINING

My family and friends convinced me to enter the contest. My father took a boxing recording I had made with "Furby" Luis Alberto Martínez (commentator and friend) at the Coliseum Arena when we were students at The Raúl del Campo.

A month later they called me on the phone and told me that I was one of the fifteen finalists among the 600 competitors nationwide. I was told that I had to report to the Sheraton Hotel in Reforma. On September 1, 2000 I appeared at the press conference chaired by Javier Alarcón (the Director of Televisa Deportes) and with people from the XEQ, who would broadcast live the the contest final. That night they explained the rules of the contest and I met the other fourteen colleagues (I never saw them as opponents), among them, Ricardo Díaz, who is now a good friend of mine. Alarcón told us that we would participate in the contest with the sport in which we put our recording, which was a big problem for me because I had not practiced box narration in two years and did not have any video at home to practice. That night I returned from dinner and started practicing with my eyes closed for three hours in the bathroom of my parents' house (so as not to wake them up); from 12 to 3 am. The next day I had to be in the studio of Televisa Deportes at 7 in the morning. I set out to do things right without getting nervous, if someone beat me I was fine, he would be better than me and I would accept it.

FROM DE MICROPHONE TO THE CLASSROOM

By 12 o'clock in the day, after two rounds of narration, there were five finalists left and by 2 o'clock in the afternoon, as a surprise, but with great satisfaction, the jury of the contest had declared me the winner. Now, my problem was to notice Barter that I had to travel to Sydney, Australia.

That same afternoon I had a party at my house, family and friends gathered to celebrate. I was actually ground, I had slept three hours the night before and my Sunday was going to be very busy. On Sunday, December 3, I appeared for the first time on television in the program "Más Deporte", where I met Enrique "Perro" Bermúdez (a great guy), and in the evening I participated in the program "En la Jugada" with Raúl Orvañanos and Javier Alarcón.

On the Monday I arrived in Barter, all my teammates knew about the contest. Barbara told me that she gave me two weeks of vacation and that she knew I was going to win (something that even I didn't think would happen). During the next two weeks I realized the impact that television has, people who are looking for you to get some benefit, attend exclusive places and let you in without any problem. My father wisely told me that I should be the humble, media promotes you as a product and you know what? he was right.

EFFECTIVE TRAINING

I would arrive in Sydney already started the games because the U.S. Embassy took time to give me the visa and although I was traveling to Australia, I had to make a flight connection in Los Angeles. On Sunday, September 24, I arrived in Sydney after twenty-two hours that had passed since I entered Mexico City International Airport. The next day I was registered at the Press Media Center to accredit me, there I met Ana Guevara, who curiously had qualified for the final of the 400 meters and whose result I did not know because I was in flight. At that time there were no smart phones and access to the internet was more complicated. It was Ana herself who informed me that she had finished in fifth place (four years later it would be silver in Athens).

My instance in Sydney had unforgettable experiences, I attended finals of Athletics, Diving, Tennis, Baseball, Basketball, Tae Kwon Do and Football. I had to see two Mexicans receive medals. My work schedule was to go to events, at noon eat at the Press Center, record the daily radio program with Javier Alarcón and Anselmo Alonso from 4 to 6 in the afternoon, and then attend events until 11 at night to return to the hotel to rest. The people in Australia were very friendly, noble and sincere. There is a lot of order and they make you feel great. Work was what I had dreamed of since I was a child, but something was not right. As the days went by I missed my job at Barter more and I didn't feel satisfied. The days in Sydney helped me to realize that my true job was in the classroom and not on the microphone. Being in an Olympic Games and with the most important television company in Mexico was a privilege, however, although you are in front of a microphone and millions of people listen to you, in realized, at that moment thar you only interact with your colleagues and the production staff. I'm not going to criticize the work of a journalist and sports commentator, but I realized that my work must be more human, learn, teach, develop, create and make decisions and that was not going to happen as a commentator, at least, for many years.

I returned to Mexico and when I appeared in Barter everyone thought I would quit my job. However, from there, I became more involved with the company and in generating more benefits with my work.

After several weeks, Javier Alarcón asked to speak with me. The decision before attending the meeting was already made, I thanked him and from that moment, my career as a sports commentator was over.

The 9 months I had been in Barter and the 2 weeks I was in Sydney opened my eyes to realize that I had been a "commentator by conviction", but in reality I was a "trainer by vocation", I had always been, nothing else, but I had not noticed it.

EFFECTIVE TRAINING

FROM DE MICROPHONE TO THE CLASSROOM

"Voices Draft" Finalists

Box Narration

EFFECTIVE TRAINING

Sídney Olympic Games 2000
"Mens Tennis Final"

Radio Program
With Javier Alarcón and Anselmo Alonso

CHAPTER 2
TRAINING BASICS

What is a course for? It is the first question we must ask ourselves before developing a content and offering a training service.

Many companies see training as an expense and not as an investment and why do you think so? Because on many occasions courses are developed and taught without analyzing the objective of the same and the problems that exist in companies. When that happens, the course does not work and the top management of the company decides that it is not necessary to invest time, money and effort in training. That does not mean that the training does not work, the reasons why a course was needed were simply not detected and the final objective will not be accomplished.

For training to be effective it is necessary to analyze and understand the following basic concepts:

1) Elements of the Training.
2) Setting Objectives.
3) Information Collection
4) Training Needs Diagnosis.
5) Technical Training Proposal.
6) Actions That Are Done Before a Course

1. TRAINING ELEMENTS

In order for a training course to be carried out, the following elements must be available:

- **Objetive:** A course should always have a reason for being and a goal to cover.

- **Problem or situation acts**: A course will serve to cover needs, develop skills and solve problems of a current situation.

- **Information:** Every course that is taught must transmit information to the participant. The information represents the body of the course.

- **Resources:** To organize, develop and teach a course it is necessary to have both material and economic resources.

- **People to train:** A course is aimed at a number of participants and these are the ones who will receive the training.

- **Instructor:** The person in charge of delivering the training course.

2. GOAL SETTING

A goal is a short- or medium-term goal. A training objective will tell us why we need to teach a course. Before developing a course, it is necessary that the objective of training is very clear, both for those who teach the course, and for those who receive it.

The main objectives in any training course are:

1. Prepare staff for the execution of the various particular tasks of the organization.

2. Provide opportunities for continued personal development, not only in their current positions, but also for other functions for which the person may be considered.

3. Change the attitude of people with several purposes, among which are to create a more satisfactory climate among employees, increase their motivation and make them more receptive to supervision and management techniques.

The minimum requirement for a training course is that training be conducted on a regular, recurring and routine basis.

You can also solve problems through training, or set goals that are intended to achieve goals never before achieved.

From the point of view of an organization, the main objective of a course (whether in the short or medium term) is that the individual who takes it increases their productivity.

From the point of view of a participant taking a course, the main objective is to be informed, learned and developed.

From the point of view of a trainer, the main objective of a course is that the participant who takes it, meets the established objectives of the course and above all that he applies what he has learned in his daily tasks.

3. INFORMATION COLLECTION

The content is essential for there to be a quality course. However, it is very important to have different sources from which to get the information.

From the information that is obtained, what best suits the audience to which the course will be directed is chosen.

The information collected is reflected in the training manual and at the end of it is established in the "bibliography" from which the information was extracted.

Where is information collected from to teach a course? From various sources such as:

A. Books

Books are one of the main sources of information for the development of a manual. It is important to have a balance when researching information through a book. The content of it should not be copied literally (although this saves time), since it is plagiarism and is immoral and illegal conduct. Nor should the content be based on reading many books and only use this source as exclusive material, since it will take too long to complete your content and you will be too ineffective in your work. A course must take a maximum of three months from the time its preparation is approved and its objective is established to be completed and ready to be taught.

B. Newspapers and Magazines

Newspapers can be useful, as articles, data or textual statements can be extracted from there. The information obtained from this source is complementary, not the main one.

C. Internet

The internet is a very important source, as you can find very specific and varied information to complement your training content. From here you can get theoretical, practical, statistical, imagery and graphic information. What is very important is that you validate the information you obtained and verify that this information is correct. Unfortunately, on the Internet there are many pages that have erroneous or false information, for this reason, you must always verify the authenticity of the source.

D. Internal Documents and data from the company

From the company where you work, you can use manuals, policies, procedures and presentations that can be used to reinforce the content of our course, especially if the course you are going to teach is technical and focused on the internal operation of the company.

E. Surveys

You can complement you training content by doing questionnaires and tests to the staff, the results will serve to reinforce our research. It is very common to do a survey to detect training needs, we will call it DNC. In this chapter we will analyze it in detail.

TRAINNING BASICS

F. Interviews

You may interview some of the company's internal staff such as directors, managers or operational staff to obtained specific information of the operation, whether it is done correctly or incorrectly. This will help you to establish the desirable behaviors that are required to be trained.

G. Field Observation

A field observation consists of seeing and analyzing a person's work in their position. Let's assume that you are developing a course of "Induction to the Position of an Account Executive in a Bank". In you observation you will analyze what they do with customers?, how do they serve them? Both face to face, and by telephone. From there you will take the best performed behaviors, analyze the failures and validate this with the leader or manager of the area to obtain the desirable functions and activities that you will transmit during the course.

H. Meetings

The meetings will help you to validate the information obtained and make corrections and improvements to your content.

4. TRAINING NEEDS DIAGNOSIS

If you work within a company, the first thing you have to do is a diagnosis of training needs, better known in the medium as TND.

What is a TND?

It is the procedure from which information is obtained necessary to develop training plans and programs in organizations for the strengthening of knowledge, skills or attitudes of employees.

¿When to do a TND?
When there is:
- Problems in the organization.
- Deviations in productivity.
- Failure to meet goals.
- Cultural changes, in policies, methods or techniques.
- Low or high staff.
- High staff turnover.
- Repeated absenteeism.
- Changes of function or position.
- Staff requests.
- Poor operation of machines and work equipment.

TRAINNING BASICS

- Rejection of products.
- Non-existent work procedures.
- Poor worker performance.

How to make a TND?

There are four questions that the TND should allow to obtain:

- Who needs training?
- What do they need training in?
- With what level of depth?
- When and in what order should they be trained?

The methods for obtaining the information are diverse, but the most common are interviews, questionnaires and "Focus Groups".

A. Interviews

Questions are asked of the interviewee and the interviewer takes note and records them, either in audio or video. From that interview you will make conclusions.

B. Questionnaires

The questionnaires are usually made in writing or electronically, they are uploaded to a platform for the respondent to answer. Questionnaires may have open-ended, closed-ended, or multiple-choice questions.

C. Focus Group

It is a technique to obtain qualitative data necessary for an investigation. This information is achieved by bringing together a small group of six to twelve people in order to present their opinions and preferences around a product, a service, an idea, an advertisement, a content or a course.

5. TECHNICAL TRAINING PROPOSAL

To teach a course, it is first necessary to submit a technical proposal to the Human Resources area for prior authorization.

If you work in an external consultancy, this proposal will be presented to your client, If you work within a company that requires internal training, you will present it, either to the person in charge of the training area or Human Resources and if the company is small, to the General Director.

What should a technical training proposal include?

- **Background:** It refers to a brief description of the company or area to be investigated, in which mention is made of the current problem for which it is necessary to teach a course.

TRAINNING BASICS

- **Training objective:** The goal to be achieved at the end of a course.

- **Content:** It is the structure of the course. It refers to the main chapters, topics and subtopics that the course content will cover.

- **General conditions:** It refers to the policies, norms and rules that must be followed in order to teach the course and meet the established objectives.

- **Investment:** It is the amount of money that will be invested to carry out the session. This includes money spent on materials, logistics, etc.

- **Logistics:** It refers to all the activities and processes prior to carrying out a training course.

It is recommended to present this proposal in a Power Point presentation and accompany it with illustrations or photographs to make it more friendly to the eye.

Later in this book we will see the way in which a presentation is designed and elaborated.

6. ACTIONS THAT ARE DONE BEFORE A COURSE

So far already identified what is needed to give a course, its objective, where we collect information, how to make a DNC and a technical proposal, but something very important is missing ... The authorization or approval of our course proposal.

If we do not receive the authorization, the course cannot be carried out.

What is done once the course is authorized?

- Schedule training activities.
- Develop a manual.
- Prepare a presentation.
- Develop a checklist of materials.

Later, in another chapter, we will explain in detail each of these four stages that will help us prepare and develop the course.

TRAINNING BASICS

CHAPTER 3
STORY
"FROM THE SUMMIT TO THE PRECIPICE"

After I retired as a commentator, things continued to improve day by day. Barter began to have an accelerated growth, with the merger of BarterTrust grew exponentially.

When I started we were less than 20 people and we only worked in the middle of a floor of a building located next to Periférico Sur, in Mexico City. Months after the merger we had two full floors and we were more than 100 people who worked there. The Human Resources area hired two more people in Recruitment, so in the area we were six people. Enrique Enciso became President of Latin America and hired Alejandro Mariani, a new Administrative Manager who months later would be the new CEO. The company was also strengthened with the hiring of Ricardo Kawagi, as Commercial Director. At the international level, a new CEO was hired, a very young Englishman with new ideas. In addition, an office was opened in Sao Paulo, Brazil, which depended on the office in Mexico.

However, not everything was doing well, since Bárbara Chaparro, my direct boss, left the company due to differences with Enrique. That led to Jaqueline being appointed Recruitment Manager and me, Training Manager. The funny thing is that when I started I reported to Ricardo

Sainz and now he would report to me. This must have been a very difficult situation for him and soon quit his job.

With my new responsibility as Training Manager and the growth of the company I had to make important changes. By then I was reporting directly to the CEO, Alejandro Mariani, but much of my work and work development was due to Alicia Enciso, who was still with the company as an advisor. She taught me to work by goals, a situation I continue doing throught this day.

The first thing that was done and that was not had, was to establish the objectives of the Human Resources and Training area. We improved the Induction program, which had a theoretical presentation of the exchange system, a practical method to learn from the platform and then, a one-week training system so that the sales staff could be effective from their entry in a period of two weeks.

All training was translated into English for use in other BarterTrust offices and also into portuguese for the Sao Paulo office. Thanks to this I began to give my first courses in another language other than Spanish.

In those months I learned to make a "Training Needs Diagnosis" (TND) to start developing an Organizational Development program with the staff of the institution. I learned to work by competencies and to plan courses based on them.

But my work not only focused on the training part, but I also began to learn various HR tasks such as: Recruitment, Graphology, Personnel Management, Work Environment and Job Description. Little by little, as the months went by, Jaqueline and I covered all the functions of the Human Resources area.

When a company grows, it has more revenue, but more problems came also and one of the most common is that of communication. For the first time since I had finished my degree (outside of my work as a commentator), I had the opportunity to implement concepts and actions of internal communication. To this end, a communication board was created to report on the main news of the medium. There was a large dining room on the ground floor, which had ping pong and table football. Convivialities were made every two months with all the employees of the office and these were paid with a fund that was joined with the unpunctual employees. Simply put, everything was going very well, I couldn't be happier about my stay at BarterTrust.

However, almost everything that goes up fast, tends to go down fast and BarterTrust was no exception.

The company internationally began to spend more money than it generated. Moving the headquarters from San Francisco to London (where the CEO lived), using a new technology platform for all customers caused many millions of dollars to be spent. Few months later, several offices closed and the Mexico office had the problem that it was the subsidiary of the Sao Paulo office.

Enrique and Alicia Enciso left the company and with them little by little, the staff of the Mexico office was weakened. Now, the office was run by Alejandro Mariani and Ricardo Kawagi, whose working relationship with both was excellent. However, little by little the dismissals began due to economic problems, which generated fear and demotivation in the staff. A Work Environment Survey was carried out, all staff contracts were updated and put in order. That situation left people a little calmer, but it didn't help to avoid the economic problems the company was going through.

All training projects were halted. By 2002 instead of 100, there were just under 20 people working. The Mexico office had been separated from BarterTrust International and the Sao Paulo office closed. In Human Resources it was only Jaqueline and I. Fortunately, I did not have to make effective thelayoffs, a situation that was complicated to handle.

Finally, in February 2002 and by mutual agreement, we decided both parties to end the employment relationship with BarterTrust. The departure was on very good terms and there was a bond of cordiality with Ricardo and Alejandro.

Jaqueline, today, is still a great friend and she was my partner in these complicated months. I saw Enrique and Alicia Enciso a couple of times, also with a lot of respect and gratitude.

BarterTrust for me was a great school, my first job in training that gave me satisfaction and my first blows. But it was much more positive than the negative situations and learning. At that time I was starting my professional development in the training, but I still had a lot to learn and execute.

After my departure I started looking for a job again, I wasn't going back to the microphone, so I went to a lot of interviews for a job, either as an instructor or Training Manager. As a result I did poorly, as I was not hired. I mistakenly asked for much more than I earned at Barter and to be honest, I had never worked in a large corporate or had the experience I thought I had.

EFFECTIVE TRAINING

As the months went by it was more difficult for me to find a job, the more time you have without working the job environment sees you as an unwanted and unattractive person to be hired.

During those months unemployed I had some interventions as a freelance instructor. A freelancer is someone who does not work as a permanent in a company, but collaborates for several and does it by project. You can charge well, but you don't have the benefits and benefits that you have in a company.

I first worked in Organizational Development Mexico through my sister Roxana, who worked there and contacted the General Manager, José Luis Pinheiro. There I experienced for the first time working in integration events and I learned about learning through dynamics.

Bárbara Chaparro already worked as Deputy Director of Human Resources in a mortgage company. He called me and I helped his Training Manager develop a trivia game (questions and answers) to improve the training. I quoted the project and it was accepted, however, due to my inexperience, I never took into account that when you develop a product, you have frequent meetings and corrections. Finally, I worked three times as many hours as I estimated to work and the product turned out well, but not to the complete liking of Barbara and her Training Manager.

Several more months passed and I could not get a job, I felt more and more anguished and desperate. I had to sell my car to continue subsisting for a few more months.

I was no longer looking for a job where I earned more than the previous one, I was looking for a job to earn the same or less than the previous one. My economic pretensions went down because of my need, what I needed was a job. Also, when you go to interviews, if they notice that, companies offer you less or don't hire you.

My financial situation caused friction and problems with my parents and I decided to go away. I went to Cancun with a friend to try new job experiencies. My stay there was not pleasant, I had a lot of pressure to do something fast, which made me stress and sleep very little.

A month into my Cancun adventure, a former Barter partner called me on the phone. She worked at an Afore and there was a vacancy in the training area. I returned to Mexico City and in less than a week accepted the offer as a Training Analyst. I would earn a little less than at Barter, but my medium-term economic problems would disappear. This Afore was a large and important company, in which I could have job growth and more learning than in my previous experience.

After being 2 years earlier at the top in Barter, then falling to the precipice with my period of unemployment and economic problems, everything seemed to indicate that better times and great satisfactions would come.

"Well, at least that's what I believed."

Barter Year End Meal with
Alicia Enciso

Barter Year End Meal
with
Bárbara Chaparro

EFFECTIVE TRAINING

Barter Year End Meal with
Jaqueline Flores and Mónica Jimenez

BarterTrust Convention
in Taxco with Ricardo Kawagi

CHAPTER 4
PLANNING A COURSE

Once authorized, either by the Training or Human Resources area, the planning period of a course begins. Many people who have taken one think that the instructor explains slides and there is no previous work before the delivery of the same. Actually, it's quite the opposite. Teaching a course takes many hours of preparation and prior planning. The more improvised the work, the more failures and the more deficient it will be. A new, well-planned course must take at least five times the duration of the course to develop and plan. For example, an eight-hour cuso should take at least a full week to prepare, plan, and prepare.

Planning a course involves taking into account many factors, such as: objective, agenda, investment, resources (materials, number of participants, location) and logistics activities.

Planning a course involves taking into account the following:
1. Schedule activities.
2. Develop a training manual.
3. Prepare a course presentation.
4. Develop a materials checklist.
5. Call Invitation.

1. SCHEDULE ACTIVITIES

Programming a course requires many activities prior to its teaching. That is why it is advisable to do the following:

A. List all the necessary activities to be carried out before teaching the course. Let's see below some of the activities that are required to plan an already authorized course:
    - Establish the date of delivery of the course.
    - Develop a participant's manual.
    - Prepare a presentation of the course.
    - Develop exercises and dynamics of the course (if required).
    - Prepare exams (if the course requires it).
    - Develop a checklist of materials.
    - Send the call and invitations to the course.
    - See the space where the training is going to be given.

PLANNING A COURSE

- Get the projector and the screen where the course is going to be projected.

- Get coffee break of the course.

- Train the people who will support the training and training (if the course requires it, it may be that the same one who developed the course is the only instructor).

- Get all the material required by the course.

- Set up the room or space where the training will be given.

B. Subsequently, these activities must be placed within a calendar establishing the date and time of application of each of them.

A calendar of activities is very useful, especially if several people are involved in the process. In a large corporation, where there are several people in the training area, this calendar of activities may be spread over several people and each of them may be doing different activities at the same time.

2. DEVELOP A TRAINNING MANUAL

A manual is a specific document that contains all the detailed information regarding a course. The objective of preparing a manual is that after a course has been taught, the participant has the specific and detailed information to consult information or resolve doubts. The manual is not for the participant during a course to consult, but must be a reference material for after it.

A. Characteristics

A manual must have two fundamental characteristics:
- That it is clear and understandable when reading.

- That the information you are looking for is found quickly and easily.

B. Design

- It is recommended that a manual has the company logo.

- If the course has a logo or slogan it is recommended to use it.

- That it has a general cover and a cover for each title of the course.

PLANNING A COURSE

- A header at the top of each page (you can use the color of the company).

- A frame can be used inside which the course content will be written.

- Use illustrations only on covers.

- Diagrams, graphs, and charts can be included on the interior pages.

- Use legible handwriting (Helvetica, Arial or Times New Roman) bold at 12 points.

- Use a line spacing of 1.5 spaces to facilitate the reading of the document.

- Visibly put all the pages of the document in the corners.

C. **Structure**

A training manual must have the following structure:

a. Index

It is the reference that helps us to be able to find easily and quickly on which page to find a specific topic or subtopic seen during the session.

b. Objetives:

These are the objectives of the course. There may be one general goal and several specific goals.
- The general objective is the one that is sought to be achieved at the end of the training.
- The specific objectives are those that cover each of the topics that will be seen on the training course.

c. Thematic content:

These are the topics and sub-themes covered on the training course. It is the body of the manual and the basis of the entire course.

d. Conclusions or recommendations:

It is the closing of the manual where a summary of what is seen in the manual and what should be applied at work.

e. <u>Bibliography or participants in the manual:</u>
   The supporting books that were used for the manual or the participants who developed it.

Previously it was very common to make two manuals: one for the participant and the other for the instructor. The instructor's manual, in addition to the course content and the aforementioned sections, had a series of instructions on how to teach each topic and if there were dynamics or exercises, how to carry them out.

Currently it is not necessary to elaborate an instructor's manual, since if days before teaching the course an "Internal Training" is given (training session to those who will teach the course), the instructors will be perfectly prepared to give the course. An internal face-to-face training is more accurate and will always take less time than crafting an Instructor's Manual.

3. PREPARE A COURSE PRESENTATION

A course presentation is an electronic document that serves as a support to the instructor to teach a course. The goal of a presentation is to provide support to the instructor and participants. To the instructor to present their topics and to the participants to better understand what the instructor said.

A presentation must always be friendly and above all graphic, so that it is attractive to the participant. It is elaborated from the Participant Manual, it must be a summary of it, but it must also have support slides for the instructor, which are not in the manual. Slides such as:

- Presentation of the participants.
- Course Rules.
- Schedules and agenda of the course.
- Exercise or dynamic instructions.
- Reflections (if required).
- Signs of recesses.
- Closure sheet.

A. Design

- It is recommended that a manual has the company logo.

- That it has a general cover and a cover for each title of the course.

- A header at the top of each page (you can use the color of the company).

- Use illustrations or photographs in the pictures.

- Diagrams, graphs, and charts can be included on the interior pages.

- Use letter (Helvetica, Arial or Times New Roman) dark color of 24 to 20 points.

- Light background (white or any color in a very faint and light tone).

B. Structure

A training presentation must have the following structure:

a. <u>Presentation</u>

Contains the points that the instructor wants to emphasize during the presentation of the course.

b. <u>Session Rules</u>

They serve so that the instructor has greater control of the group.

c. <u>Objetives:</u>

They are the general and specific objectives of the course. The generals are which the instructor wants to achieve at the end of the course, the specific ones are those contained in each topic of the course.

d. <u>Thematic Content:</u>

These are the topics and sub-themes covered by the training. It is the body of the manual, the basis of the whole course.

e. <u>Dynamics and Exercises:</u>

The dynamics and exercises make the session more fun and also serve to measure behaviors, skills, competencies and knowledge about what has been learned.

f. <u>Breaks:</u>

It helps the instructor know when the coffee breaks will take place, the lunch time, or if the course continues the next day.

g. <u>Conclusions or Recommendations:</u>

It is the closing of the course where a summary of what has been seen and what should be applied in the day to day work is indicated.

A presentation must have an impeccable visual appearance, since it is the face of the instructor before his audience. It is very important to check that the presentation does not contain errors or spelling mistakes. Nor should the presentation be saturated with text, since after a while the participant's got eyestrain and can generate a lack of attention.

4. DEVELOP A MATERIAL CHECKLIST

It is a list of all the necessary material that the instructor must need to able to teach in a course. It is important to always have a checklist format on hand before teaching a course.

For this checklist it is advisable to use the Microsoft Excel program, since it divides us into columns the list of what we need to have for a course.

Some of the main materials that are used in any training course are:
- Projector
- Flat white screen or a white clear wall
- Computer or laptop
- Electrical extension
- Electrical Multicontact Connections
- White labels
- Markers
- Flipchart or blackboard sheets
- Pens
- White sheets
- Attendance List
- Participant Manual
- Course Evaluations

EFFECTIVE TRAINING

Below is an example of a checklist for a course:

Material request date:	**07-jun**
Course delivery date:	**22-jun**
Number of participants: approx.	**20**
Material delivery date:	**10-jun**
Course Name:	Time Management
Person responsible for material:	GS
Place where the course will be taken:	Mexico City

Material for Participants	
Quantity	Material Description
3	Attendance Lists
20	Diplomas

EXTRA MATERIAL	
Quantity	Material Description
1	Cutters
1	Masking Tape
22	White labels presentation
20	Evaluations
50	White Sheets
8	markers of different colors
1	Course Presentation
20	Pens
1	Remote Control with Lasser Pointer
1	Camera
4	Batteries
1	Speaker
1	suitcase

5. CALL INVITATION

Attendance at a course may be voluntary or mandatory. For both cases, a call invitation must be made at least one week in advance so that participants can organize their time and generate a space in their agenda for the date of the established course. This call is made via email.

A call must contain all the necessary information elements. The use of these templates allows us to save time when following a script and not have to act by memory, in addition, it ensures that we will not forget in the call invitation any necessary information.

- First of the call, it is indicated who are the participants to attend the course and their direct bosses are copied.

- Secondly, we place the date on which the course will be held so that it is reserved in the agenda of the invited participants.

- Then we will put the start up time and the expected time of completion of the course.

- Then we put the place where it is going to be celebrated.

- Finally we will put the objectives of the course and the topics.

It is very important that 24 hours after the email has been sent, it is confirmed if the participants received the call and determine who will attend.

This will help us to know the amount of material that has to be obtained and the amount of sheets that must be printed as a support material.

When the course is open to the general public and is external to the company where we work, the invitation to the course is made through an internet page whose promotion of it is done through different media and on digital networks.

Purchase this book by...

Either in Kindle or Paperback formats

Joselo Arizaleta

You can also buy it in Spanish.

www.amazon.com.mx

CHAPTER 5
STORY
"MI PASSAGE THROUGH THE FINANTIAL ENVIRONMENT"

In 2003 I joined a prestigious Afore with the illusion to develop and grow in a large company.

For those who do not know, an Afore (Retirement Fund Administrator) is a private financial institution that is responsible for managing the retirement funds of workers affiliated to the Social Security. Afores administrate funds works through personal accounts that are assign to each worker, in which the contributions made throughout their working life are deposited.

My first week was training, my first day with an induction course and the other days taking a course that is taught to the promoters to know the laws of the that rules Afores. That was the only good week I had on that place.

From there, things were very difficult. To begin with, my boss, the Training Manager was younger than me and when she realized I have proactivity and leadership, I consider that she felt that her job and position was threatened so her attitude with me changed. My job as an analyst was completely numerical, statistical, in which I had to review documents, score exams and capture information in a system. There was too much work and many activities were very repetitive. For me it started to be difficult to work because at Barter I had done much more important functions than what I was doing on the Afore.

In the organization there were many people, only in Human Resources there were more than 50 people. There was a lot of disorganization and communication problems among all.

In the training area there was another analyst, but she was given little work and I was held by the hand. When I made a job proposal, my boss presented it to the Human Resources Director as her idea, so my work had no credit.

Little by little I began to have differences and arguments more frequently with my boss. Part of it was also my fault, I was very competitive at that time and my character was strong and sometimes explosive.

Every day that passed I wanted to get out of there, but I did not want to live again the stage of unemployment.

Later I requested to do a Field Research to see how the promoters, the assistants and their Branch Managers worked, this in order to create a specific training oriented to the position.

After that investigation I realized a sad reality: in a branch there were more than 30 promoters and only the manager and the assistant had the right tools to work. There was a computer and a phone for all the promoters, no one supported them in anything. Promoters earned minimum wage and would only earn for their commissions. Unfortunately, in less than three months, more than 80% of promoters quite to their jobs.

In meetings I always heard the Human Resources Director to comment that more staff had to be hired and that the one that was hired was not enough. To give us an idea, this Afore hired around 300 new people in a month. And a month later, at least half of them were leaving. That's how it happened every month. I told my boss and the Deputy Director of Human Resources that this had to change and that we should focus on developing people and retaining them, so that there would be no more resignations.

Analyzing in detail the Manual of the Course to Promoters I understood everything. Under the law that was in effect at the time, anyone could change Afore whenever they wanted, but once they entered a new Afore, people could not changed to another Afore after a year. All the personnel hired by Afore as promoters were asked for a single requirement, that when they entered they registered in that Afore; this ensured the resources of each employee for at least one year.

So I can tell you that the recruitment was a hoax, it was actually a sale disguised as recruitment, with false promises, since this Afore was not interested in retaining or developing its promoters, only to stay and manage its retirement fund.

I really felt ashamed and angry, I was in a nightmare and I didn't want to be part of a company that worked and treated people like that.

That's how a miracle came about, Bárbara Chaparro called me to offer me the position of instructor in a mortgage company. I went to two interviews and they finally accepted me. I returned to the Afore and submitted my resignation, which was accepted, although I was not given my settlement at that time. It was not until a month later and with the threat of a labor lawsuit when they gave me the check that covered my settlement. The nightmare of my stay in this Afore had become eternal, it only lasted three months, but, finally, it was over.

In November 2003 I joined Hipotecaria Nacional, a solid, stable and honest company. A mortgage company is a financial institution that is dedicated to granting loans to people for the purchase of land or a house. At that time, banks were not yet involved in the mortgage sector, so Hipotecaria Nacional was one of the two largest companies in its field in Mexico.

MI PASSAGE TRHOUGH THE FINANTIAL ENVIRONMENT

Barbara introduced me to my new boss, Gloria Gómez Palacio. I have a great appreciation for her and Oscar Ávila, since they gave me the freedom to land my ideas, but above all, I learned a lot from them in terms of leadership and strategy.

In Hipotecaria Nacional many things needed to be developed and fortunately, most of the time I always had the approval to do it with his supervision and good communication.

The wonderful thing about the world of training is that to teach, you first have to learn and that's what I did for the next three months. Know first in detail how a mortgage works, how is the process for a mortgage loan, what are the key areas involved in the process, how a branch office works.

In Human Resources there was a lot of union and that was thanks to Bárbara Chaparro, who promoted coexistence in the area. Unfortunately she work only two more months after my entry and then quit her job, but part of his integrating work between the areas of Human Resources, remained independent of the new director who entered months later.

Throughout this process I met Mary Rodriguez, a person who had worked in branch offices She was one of the first employees in the company, and was very proactive and charismatic.

With everything I learned from Mary I was able to start structuring specialized courses to different positions. First a "General Induction" was made and then more specialized courses began to be given to different areas, such as Legal, Branch Office, Administrative and Human Resources.

Part of the courses I developed, the other part, the experts of the corresponding area. The Training area had seven people, including me. There was an assistant director (Gloria), a manager, (Oscar), two instructors, a coordinator and me as another instructor. The truth was not easy and we did not always work well as a team; starting with me, although I was developing many proyects, I was very competitive and did not help and hard to work on a team. My competitive attitude slowed down the work of others. Years later I would change my vision completely.

Something very satisfying in Hipotecaria Nacional was that I was able to create courses and develop programs. I substantially improved the way I taught courses and learned to sense group attitudes. I started to experience the first courses by e-learning.

I also learned to negotiate with other areas in meetings to provide training for both parties to benefit, I owe that to Oscar, who was very good at it.

MI PASSAGE TRHOUGH THE FINANTIAL ENVIRONMENT

At that time there was a lot of communication by email, but there was no intranet page, in addition, our area was in another building several blocks from the corporate, so our work if it did not have much impact and was not perceived as we wanted by the other areas. For that reason I decided to promote the activities of the training area in all the Communication Boards of the main building of the corporate, which we did on a monthly basis.

In Training we always had a lot of work to do, there were enough staff to take it forward. Unfortunately, the number of courses that the other areas needed were not taught. As a message to readers, believe me it is very important to learn. In the training business, the one who succeeds is the one who learns, but the one who learns continuously. Many times we focus on the problems of the area, the meetings, the opinions, but if you do not learn the operation of the company in which you work and update yourself, you can not contribute what you need. It is true that this requires time and can slow down our other tasks, but in the end, that learning applied to daily work and generates much greater impact on individual work, to the area and to the organization.

Sometimes our area and Human Resources saw us as the "ugly duckling" of the organization, but I am sure that if all the area learn more and contributes more to the operation, that situation would have changed.

EFFECTIVE TRAINING

During 2004 a new Training Manager, Antonio Mendoza, came to work with us, who became more involved in the operation and was a great support to my work. I must admit that I was very demotivated by his entry, since I aspired to that position, but Gloria was right, I was not mature enough to exercise it correctly. Years later I would realize this.

At the end of 2004 we were given the news that BBVA Bancomer had bought Hipotecaria Nacional, which generated a lot of uncertainty and insecurity in all of us. Little by little the changes in the organizational structure began and I realized that if I didn't do something, if I didn't move, I would soon be out of my job. One thing is for sure, there were not going to be two areas of Human Resources in Bancomer and the logical thing was that the Human Resources area of Hipotecaria Nacional was going to disappear or at least, many people of the area would no longer have a place in the organization.

Hipotecaria Nacional taught me to develop programs (something that at Barter I had neither the time nor the budget to do), impact on the training of many more people, learn to negotiate and obtain information from other areas. But I also have a lot to do and to change: temper my character, learn to work as a team, lead people and bring out the best in others.

Personally, this institution also gave me friendships that I value. For many years I kept in touch with Oscar and Gloria, in addition, I now have two great friends in Sandra Alegría (Training Analyst) and Adriana Trenado (Compensation Manager).

At that time I went to several interviews and there was a consultancy that caught my attention, combining sport and training. The economic proposal and the position were very attractive.

It was time for a change, Hipotecaria had been a great experience, but my moment was no longer there. I was about to make a decision that would change my life forever.

EFFECTIVE TRAINING

MI PASSAGE TRHOUGH THE FINANTIAL ENVIRONMENT

Diploma Ceromony in Hipotecaria Nacional

Víctor Manuel Requejo
Founder of Hipotecaria Nacional

Hipotecaria Nacional Corporate Bulding, before being adquired by BBVA Bancomer

Hipotecaria Nacional Branch Office, after the adquisition from BBVA Bancomer

CHAPTER 6
LEARNING

From the moment a human being is born, he or she begins to learn. It is a natural, innate, and evolutionary ability of the human race. Since we are babies we learn to identify smells, recognize our parents, know what we like and what we don't. Subsequently, we learn to walk and then to speak. This whole process continues throughout our lives. However, over the years, the will to learn does not remain the same in everyone and little by little this skill decreases, but it never stops being.

The human being only uses 10% of his brain capacity and geniuses and great characters, such as Einstein, Newton or Stephen Hawking employed a little more.

It is very important for an instructor who is going to explain the content of a course, to make sure that everyone understands what the instructor explained; for this it is essential that you understand how human beings learn, all humans do not learn in the same way or with the same ease or at the same speed.

It is true that an adult requires a positive attitude to learn, but the instructor must be a facilitator of that learning.

1. THE TEACHING AND LEARNING PROCESS

For the teaching-learning process to take place, there must always be a participant. An instructor is not always necessary, since learning can be self-taught, the participant researching and reading on their own to learn.

But if the course is given in a training classroom, there will always be two elements, the instructor and the participant.

The teaching-learning process in a classroom is as follows:

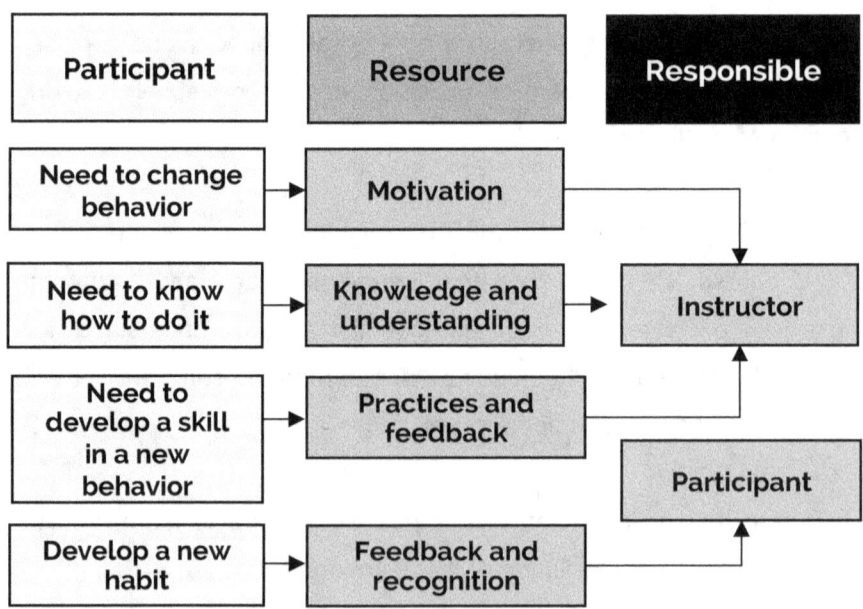

LEARNING

2. PARTICIPANT LEARNING

To be more effective in training it is necessary to know the ways in which a participant learns the information they receive during a course.

The participant learns through two ways:

A. Learning through Reasoning,

To understand this type of learning you first have to know the structure in which our brain thinks. The brain is divided into two hemispheres: the left and the right.

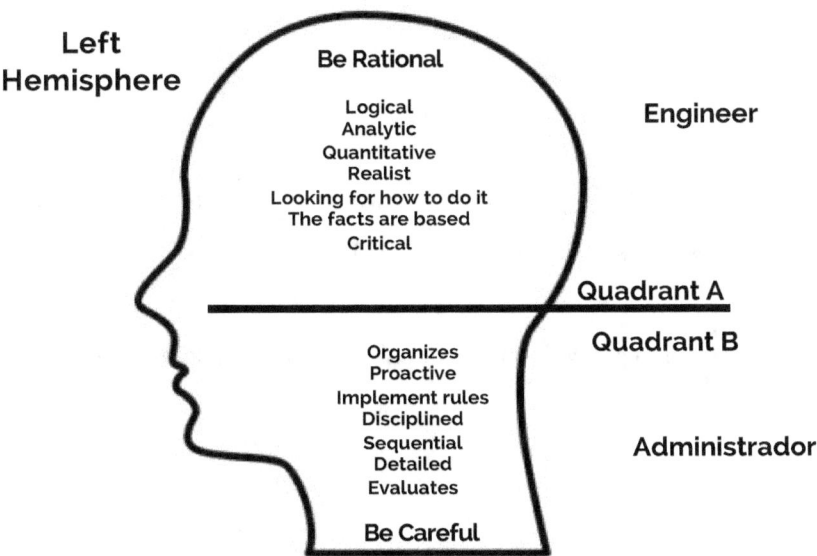

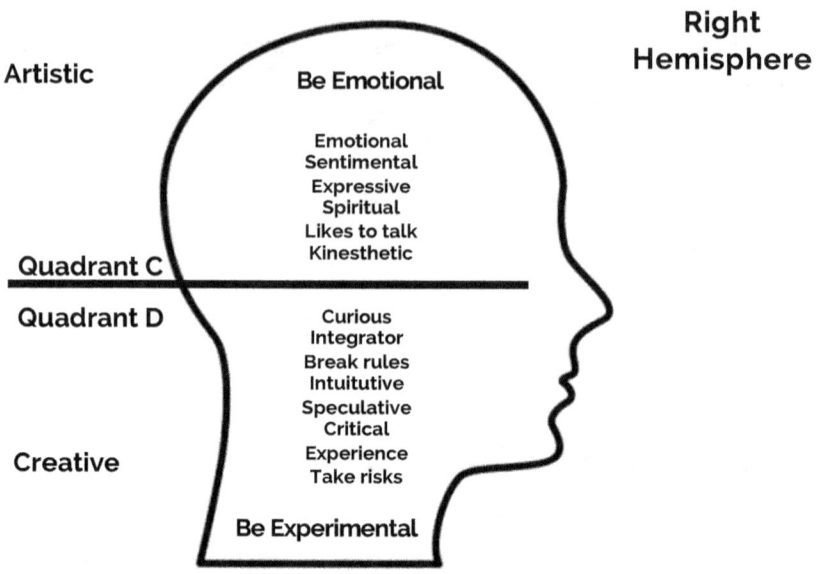

B. Learning through the Senses

To understand this type of learning we must first know the way we learn and perceive the world around us through the senses.

Sensory learning is divided into: visual, auditory and kinesthetic.

LEARNING

a. <u>Visual</u>

They are the ones who need to see and be looked at. These types of people are fast, so much so that when speaking they can omit words because of the speed of their thinking, it is as if thought wins over the word. They usually have a loud voice volume. They think of images that represent ideas. They can create images of several ideas at the same time, move those images around the central theme, put them in sequence, add more images to it, join two images to make a new one; the speed with which images change allows them to think about several things at the same time. Because of that same speed, sometimes it seems that the reasoning does not end, because in his head a new image has appeared that has totally displaced the previous one.

b. <u>Auditory</u>

With an intermediate rhythm, they make a small pause when speaking, such as: mmm, aha, they need to know that the other is understanding or, at least, listening. Thought parallels what they hear or speak. They tend to be deeper than visuals, but encompassing fewer things.

They are usually conversationalists and do not always look at the interlocutor, but give preference to the auditory field. They use abstract ideas well. Their thinking is linear, one idea continues to the other, for that reason it can bother them when they change topics without having finished dealing.

c. <u>Kinesthetic</u>

They need more physical contact and are very sensitive. Their world is sensations, mainly at the skin level. The affective aspect and emotions are very important to them. In this thought process they use abstract images and ideas and from time to time, they become abstracted in a subject. They have an intuition that allows them to reach conclusions without having performed a complete logical analysis.

The way in which a course is taught is very important, since it depends on how much the participant learns. That is why a presentation must contain elements that facilitate learning for both those who have predominance of the cerebral and right hemispheres. It must also contain visual, auditory and kinesthetic elements.

3. ACCELERATED LEARNING TECHNIQUES

There are several techniques that can help the participant learn faster. These techniques are:

A. Mind Map

A mind map is a diagram used to represent the words, ideas, tasks, or other concepts linked and arranged around a keyword or a central idea. It is used for the generation, visualization, structure, taxonomic classification of ideas and as an internal aid for study, planning, organization, problem solving, decision making and writing.

It is also familiarly known as concept map. A mind map is a technique used for the graphical representation of knowledge, therefore a concept map is a network of concepts. In the network, nodes represent the concepts, and the links represent the relationships between the concepts.

The mind maps were developed by Professor Joseph D. Novak of Cornell University in 1960, based on David Ausubel's theories of meaningful learning. According to Ausubel, "the most important factor in learning is what the subject already knows." Therefore, meaningful learning occurs when a person consciously and explicitly links those new concepts to others he already possesses. When this significant learning occurs, a series of changes occur in our cognitive structure, modifying existing concepts and forming new links between them.

Mind Map

B. **Flowchart**

It is the graphical representation of the algorithm or process. It is used in disciplines such as programming, economics, industrial processes and cognitive psychology.

An activity diagram represents the step-by-step, business and operational workflows of the components in a system.

LEARNING

These diagrams use symbols with defined meanings that represent the steps of the algorithm and represent the execution flow by arrows that connect the process start and end points.

Flowchart

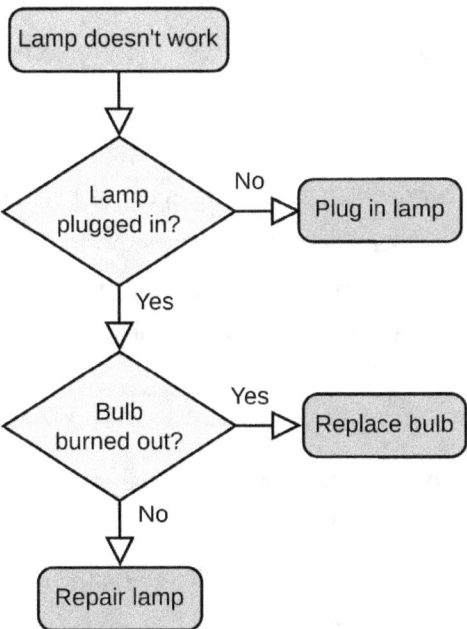

C. Group Dynamics

Group dynamics have been called "games" because they are fun and engaging for people and because they are fictional.

The dynamics for groups acquire a specific value of fun that not only stimulate emotionality and creativity, but also introduce dynamism and positive tension in the groups. The character of the game also contains a double aspect:

- It implies the fact of dissociating oneself from the serious situation of the moment.
- Achieves a deep identification with the problems with which you work.

By the way, the proposition of a game is usually linked to a change in the medium of interaction. The most important thing is that the character of play integrates the six essential components of the human being: corporeal, affective, cognitive, social, aesthetic and spiritual.

The dynamics for groups have also been called "experiential", because they make you live or feel a real situation. Which is very important, education becomes formative and ceases to be informative to become experiential knowledge.

Group dynamics provide experiences in the form of games so that people can get the most out of the experience.

Group dynamics are also called "structured experiences" because they are designed based on real-world experiences that are structured for learning purposes. What is sought is that people experience the fact as if it were actually happening.

Group Dynamics

D. **Videos**

The video is a mass dissemination medium aimed at a homogeneous audience, with common interests, which is usually concentrated in a certain place for its projection, accompanied by oral presentations and debates, among others, which favors that its filmmakers have an immediate feedback of their work.

This characteristic fundamentally establishes the difference with film and television, which is aimed at a more heterogeneous audience, where feedback is not immediate. But the most important dimension to highlight in video is that it can be used as an important audiovisual means of teaching, since it combines elements of other media, such as photography, moving image, text and sound in order to favor the development of the teaching-learning process.

Videos

The didactic video is a communication media that has its own language, whose sequence induces the receiver to synthesize feelings, ideas, conceptions, etc., which can reinforce or modify those that he had previously. It allows to methodize actions and approaches, the use of techniques, recompose and synthesize actions and reactions, as well as capturing and reproducing exceptional real situations that can be carefully studied and analyzed at different times.

LEARNING

¡The solution you need!

Look for us at:

 contacto@solderh.com

 www.solderh.com

 solderhconsultoría

 SOLDERH

CHAPTER 7
STORY
"CONSULTANCY AND SPORTS"

In April 2005 I joined the Spanish consultancy Make a Team, which was owned by Jorge Valdano, a cultured and prepared former Argentine football (soccer) player who founded his company with the aim of training people, always relating his leadership philosophy with sport.

Valdano was a successful football player, although technically he was not gifted, his intelligence, attitude and header made him stand out as a quality center forward. He played for Real Madrid and was world champion in Mexico 86 with the Argentina national team alongside Diego Armando Maradona. After he retired as a footballer he worked as a coach, to then be Sports Director and finally, General Director of Real Madrid.

In 1999 and after collaborating with the prestigious consultancy Ernst & Young, Jorge Valdano created with Juan Antonio Corbalán, Andoni Zubizarreta and the consultant Juan Mateo, the first Spanish company that built bridges between the world of sport and management in Spain: MakeaTeam. This company was a pioneer in the research and development of equipment, and soon became a prestigious consultancy both in Spain and in Latin America.

EFFECTIVE TRAINING

A consultancy is an organization that offers a specialized professional service with specific knowledge in an area, which advises other companies. In the case of MakeaTeam, it advised and provided solutions to other companies with training courses and events with team building activities.

The Mexico office had twelve people: three managers, eight consultants and a courier. From my first day I was taken to a course that was being taught to managers of The Santander Bank in a prestigious hotel in Mexico City.

I went to that course as an observer. The course was taught by two instructors: Luis Farias and Julio Calvillo. Because of my outgoing personality and protagonist, it was very difficult for me to remain silent and not intervene. What I did do was take note of the positive and negative aspects of the course, since I had to deliver a report to the Sales Manager, Alberto Hurtado, who was my boss. The course was long, lasted three days and the participants left very happy.

When I delivered my report to Alberto, there were more negative things than positive. My report completely criticized the way in which the course was given, the games, the dynamics and the noise that was generated. But it was normal, I was used to working and giving courses with the classic expository methodology where the instructor only reads and explains the pictures of a presentation.

CONSULTANCY AND SPORTS

It took me six months to get used to a new way of working and teaching a course. Before I joined MakeaTeam I already knew how to prepare a course, make content, teach it and make a report at the end. But now, the contents were focused on issues of skills and human development.

The way of teaching was always in pairs, which always promoted teamwork. At the beginning it was very difficult for me to adapt to it, I learned that in a team the important thing is not to be the star, but to achieve very competitive results by adding complementary efforts and skills. I can be very good at something, but there are things that cost me work; if I do it alone, I will limit myself and not achieve the desired goal. On the other hand, even if it is very good for something, if I ask for the support of my partner who is good for something else in which I am not, we will both get benefits.

Another radical change that was new to me was the methodology, the courses in this consultancy were based on dynamics, reflections and theoretical framework. Normally, 50% of the time was dedicated to dynamics, 20% to reflections and the other 30% to the content or theoretical framework. This new methodology I learned is very effective, since the participant learns by living the experience and practicing it.

I started teaching a lot of courses to staff of three large international companies, such as Santander, New York Life Insurand and IXE Grupo

Financiero (now Banorte). That gave me a lot of experience in the field of teaching, made me an expert managing groups of different levels, but, above all, expanded my panorama and learning in human development issues.

I had to travel a lot and normally during my first year I went constantly to cities like: Monterrey, Guadalajara and Querétaro. Traveling is very "swell" or "cool" as my Spanish colleagues said.

Working as a team I learned the best from some of my colleagues, such as Julio Calvillo (his sense of humor applied to a course), Luis Farías (his preparation prior to a course), Mariana Ríos (his professionalism), Gaby León (to integrate audiovisuals in presentations during a course), Octavio Coronado (planning and logistics in Team Building events), Pablo Zolle (the management of dynamics) and José Luis Arizaleta (to use many examples).

During 2005 and on one of his trips to Mexico, I met Jorge Valdano. He came about three or four times a year, as he was hired by clients to give lectures. I realized his intelligence, leadership, human quality and above all, simplicity. Upon meeting him he confirmed to me that he was in the right place at the right time.

CONSULTANCY AND SPORTS

At the end of 2005 I lived one of the most satisfying moments of my professional stage. In Punta Cana, Dominican Republic, the annual convention "Golden Cirle" of Citibanamex was held. This event was an award to the branch employees who had had the best results in the year, especially the Executives and Branch Managers; in addition, deputy directors and directors of the corporate attended. The event would last three days and during the mornings, Make a Team and its team would participate with around 1,500 Banamex employees in Team Building activities. Our group was made up of twenty people, including Jorge Valdano and Spanish executives, such as Jaime Bas and Antonio Llorente. Also present were the top managers and consultants of the Mexico office, which by then, our office had grown and we had twice as many staff as when I joined. On the first day, several team building activities were carried out. For the second day there was only one dynamic, it was called the "Table Football", it was a dynamic that I adapted to a human football and whose rules I modified from a traditional football match. The dynamic was a success, the most liked of the event and would be the only dynamic that would repeat year after year in the following "Golden Circles". Jorge Valdano gave me a public recognition in front of the others and my smile I think remained, at least, a couple of days. In the end, our participation in the event was a success and Banamex opened the door for us to participate in a huge training program for all branch staff.

EFFECTIVE TRAINING

During my first year I had learned a lot in human skills, especially in relation to "Teamwork" and "Customer Service", these two I applied in my daily work and had brought me very good results until that moment.

By 2006, Make a Team began working on a huge project with Banamex. It was about providing training to all the staff of its branches throughout the country. To do this, the workforce grew and in a year, the consultancy had around 100 instructors, more than half of them as freelancers.

Working on this project personally represented me to travel a lot and in two years I was able to know almost the whole country. Beautiful places, especially Chiapas, Oaxaca and Baja

This project allowed me to meet more instructors, as was the case with Lorena Morales and Alfonso Velázquez (two of the most empathetic and talented instructors I have ever worked with).

The courses with Banamex helped us to understand how the operation of a branch works, as well as the contingencies and security systems that are in place.

CONSULTANCY AND SPORTS

During 2006 I took the course "Time Management" and later, I learned to apply it to my day to day. From there, my productivity increased. In addition to teaching courses, it gave me time to implement new projects and that began to growth within the consultancy.

One of those projects was to create an "Internal Communication Bulletin". This newsletter had different sections and would be mailed to all members of the Mexico office on a weekly basis. The purpose of that document was to notify all instructors who were constantly traveling and were short in the office about client news, changes, adjustments, policies and new projects. By 2007 it became an electronic newspaper and already had several collaborators who helped me to form it. Months later, Jaime Bas, realizing the result, asked me to coordinate with the communication people in Spain to develop a global magazine for the entire corporate.

By 2007 I could not be happier in the institution where I had learned a lot and grown professionally, however, that year I had three unpleasant anger managements moments with two consultants and a manager, who made me reflect on something that needed to change. If I continued like this, my job would go "overboard" and not only would I no longer grow, but I could lose my job.

EFFECTIVE TRAINING

My state of mind was in anger, in those three incidents, I became very aggressive with my colleagues and in front of the client Form this day until now, I think that in all three cases I was right for the differences with them, but my way of expressing and handling it was totally inadequate. I realized that fighting wasn't going to lead to anything, I had to change. A few months earlier I had already taken the course of "Assertive Communication", so I decided, as difficult as it was, to apply the "process to be assertive". It took me a lot of effort and six months of work, but I finally learned to manage my emotions and communicate them assertively.

During 2008 I took three courses and learned the basics to apply "Situational Leadership", "Coaching", and "Effective Feedback". This helped me to develop a "Training Program" for new instructors and have a group of tutors who supported me to train others. Applying this program we would have instructors prepared and ready to teach courses in the Citibanamex project in approximately one week from their entry to the company.

That project helped me to have a new promotion and now I was "Senior Consultant", one of the most experienced in the company. This would be my last ascent and from then on, my growth will stop.

CONSULTANCY AND SPORTS

By 2009 I had learned almost everything thhat MakeaTeam could teach me in terms of topics and training. When I did not travel giving courses, that year I focused more on learning in the elaboration of proposals, preparing new content, dynamics and seeing details of logistics, but, above all, my interest was in learning to sell, in becoming a "Sales Manager".

I started to have my first frustrations. One of them had to do with learning and creating new content. For example, if I wanted to research a new topic and if it wasn't sold, my research would stay on the desk. Another frustration was that I was hardly given the opportunity to attend customer appointments with Sales Managers, so I couldn't learn much on the business side and it was impossible for me to grow to the next level above my own. But, without a doubt, my biggest frustration was that of almost not having time for my personal life; during the week I traveled or was in the office and almost every Friday I traveled at night to different locations to give Banamex course on Saturday and return to Mexico City on Sunday at noon. My personal life was limited to a few hours on Sunday.

So, in August 2010 I had a meeting with Alberto Hurtado, now the General Director of the Mexico office, but we did not reach an agreement and it was then that I decided to quit my job.

It took me a month to prepare everything and deliver my position, and by September 30, 2010 my MakeaTeam adventure was over.

There were five wonderfull years and maybe a complicated one, but it was worth it. To this day I feel grateful to have worked in that consultancy and I will always consider it as my best school (above Tec de Monterrey, where I studied my career). Currently, I see several of my classmates as teachers who left me professional and life teachings.

In MakeaTeam I became an expert managing and teaching groups, I learned and applied many topics of human skills, I had a lot of fun working and now I know that learning is not fought with fun; above all, I grew and matured personally and professionally.

Like everything in life there is a process of beginning, growth, maturity, decay and end, and MakeaTeam was no exception. New challenges would come, the best work experience, until then, was over. As I said at the end of chapter 5, "working on MakeaTeam was a life-changing decision"... and it was for better.

CONSULTANCY AND SPORTS

"Golden Circle Citibanamex Convention"
in Punta Cana, Dominican Rep.
with Jorge Valdano, Antonio Llorente and Jaime Bas

"Makeateam Year End Meal"
2006 Staff

EFFECTIVE TRAINING

"Golden Circle Citibanamex Convention 2007"
In Acapulco; Mexico
"Table Football Dynamic Group"

"Golden Circle Citibanamex Convention 2007"
In Acapulco; Mexico
Makeateam Staff

CHAPTER 8
INSTRUCTOR TEACHING

First of all, do not confuse the term between consultant and instructor. Both can teach training courses, but the main difference is that the instructor is dedicated solely to the delivery of courses, while the consultant does a previous research, detects needs, creates content and also, if necessary, teaches the courses.

In this chapter we will focus on the importance of the work of the instructor, and in the next chapter we will talk about the activities of the consultant.

A good instructor is essential to the success of a course. Their knowledge, skills and experience are fundamental for their teaching to generate an impact on the participant.

Knowing the different forms of learning, we will focus on the skills that the instructor must have and the different teaching techniques that can be applied to ensure the knowledge and development of the participant.

During a course, the instructor is the center of attention for the participants; however, for him, the participants will always be the most important thing, so he must learn to manage his ego.

1. INSTRUCTOR SKILLS

For the teaching of an instructor to be effective it is necessary to have a series of skills, either innate or developed with practice. Below we will analyze these skills:

A. Focus

Always focused within the classroom, both with the participants, and with everything that happens around them.

B. Observation

Consists on having visual skills to realize everything that happens inside a classroom. An instructor will be able to identify through the view if a participant has doubts, is tired, bored or disinterested.

C. Listening

Is the ability to hear and understand the messages you receive from the audience to which you are teaching the course. From the information you perceive through listening, you can resolve doubts, give examples or give a more in-depth analysis of the topic you are exposing.

INSTRUCTOR TEACHING

D. Patience

Consists on not despairing and staying calm. The most common situations in which an instructor must be patient and remain calm occur when:

- A participant does not understand.
- A participant is reluctant to apply what is seen in the course.
- An unforeseen event arises.
- From the outside there are constant interruptions during the course.

E. Voice Volume

Speak at a high volume so that the whole group hears it. An instructor with a good voice volume will not require a microphone. A loud voice volume doesn't mean screaming.

F. Voice Tone

It is the emphasis that the instructor employs in the words he says. The tone of voice is a very useful tool to give weight and intention to the content of what is being explained. The tone of voice helps to regain the attention of a participant who has gone out of focus or attention to what is being explained.

G. Diction

It is the ability to speak in a clear way and where all words are understood thanks to a good pronunciation. A good exercise to practice diction is to read aloud with a pencil or pen in the mouth, that will accustom the tongue and lips not to open too much and will improve the diction of the interlocutor.

H. Capacity to avoid fillers

When speaking, avoid saying words such as: "this", "aha", "mjm", "ehh", etc. We make these expressions involuntarily to gain time and think during an exhibition, but they denote insecurity and lack of preparation. In addition, the muletillas take away the rhythm of our exhibition.

I. Image and presence

It refers to clothing, combing and cleanliness. It is everything that the instructor transmits of his image and reflects it in his personality.

I. Postures and gestures

It refers to the way we stand on stage, the movements of hands and feet, as well as our gesticulation and what we convey of our mood.

INSTRUCTOR TEACHING

K. **Moving on stage management**

Walking on stage is a resource to attract the attention of our audience, but in doing so we must have a balance in the use of it and not abuse this resource.

L. **Capacity to analize a group**

Any instructor, through observation and listening, will be able to analyze what happens during the course and react depending on the situation.

M. **Simple and Clear Explanations**

Speak in a way that the whole audience understands. The level of complexity and technicalities that we handle during an exhibition will depend on the degree of preparation and experience of the group with respect to the topic that will be taught.

N. **Nerve Management**

An instructor must master his nervousness and not demonstrate it to a group. The best way to do this is with practice and extensive knowledge of the subject. An instructor who cannot manage his nerves should not teach a course.

O. Honesty

An instructor must have credibility and for this, it is necessary that he is always honest. When the instructor does not know the answer to a question of the participant must accept that he does not have the information and after the course he will send him an answer. If the instructor invents the answer and the participant realizes, he will lose credibility for the remainder of the course..

P. Service Attitude

The instructor must always be at the service of the needs of the group, always keeping track of it, but always maintaining and promoting respect for others.

Q. Capacity to analize a group

An instructor, with his observation and listening, will be able to analyze what happens during the course and react depending on the situation.

- For example, if the group is tired you should do something to reactivate it or send it to a break..

- Another common example is that the group is focusing on a meaningless discussion, where it must return to the main theme.

INSTRUCTOR TEACHING

R. **Empathy**

It is the ability of the instructor to understand the way in which the participant is learning. The complex thing about a group is that not all participants learn in the same way. To generate empathy with the audience it is important to speak in a way that the entire audience understands. When giving an explanation do not lose patience and put yourself in the situation of the participant if you do not understand. The objective is not to show the participant that you know, but to facilitate the knowledge that you have of the subject.

R. **Enjoy Trainning**

When an instructor enjoys his work, he transmits this state of mind to the group and reflects them a positive attitude. It is important to show the group that you enjoy training. Try to smile, be patient and kind to the group. If you do not like to teach a course and you do it frequently, ii is better foy you to dedicate to something else.

Although some skills are innate, all will be developed with practice; the more courses the instructor teaches, the more mastery will have of his skills. An instructor of excellence is the one who is self-critical and always seeks to improve his skills.

2. TEACHING TECHNIQUES

It is very important that the instructor uses methods to communicate most effectively with the participant. Below we will see four effective techniques for the delivery of a course. These are:

A. Expository

This technique consists of communicating the ideas explaining, in detail based on slides, the topic that is being exposed.

The objectives of the Expository Technique are the transmission of knowledge, to offer a critical approach to the discipline that leads students to reflect and discover the relationships between various concepts, to form a critical mentality in the way of facing problems and the ability to choose a method to solve them..

Advantages:

- Allows you to cover wide content in a relatively short time.

- Is a good environment to make disciplines accessible to students, whose study they would find daunting if they approached them without the assistance of the instructor.

INSTRUCTOR TEACHING

- The instructor can offer a more balanced view than textbooks usually present.

- Some participants tend to learn more easily by listening than by reading.

- It facilitates the communication of information to large groups.

B. Interrogative

The instructor communicates his ideas through questions by making the participant to answers these questions and takes to the point where the instructor wants. In this case, the instructor functions as a guide or facilitator and the participant is the one who exposes the topics and content of the course.

The information is presented orally, also in order. An introduction and a brief development of the content is made.

A space of time is made for the exchange of questions and answers that serve to deepen some aspects raised in the introduction.

Advantages:

- A topic or activity starts or ends.

- Experiences, capacities, criteria of the participants are explored and it is desired to establish an adequate communication.

- There is a need to focus attention and reflect on important aspects.

- It generates in the participant greater reflection and participation.

- The participant is accustomed to thinking more about solutions and is more involved in what is being said.

C. Demostrative

The instructor communicates his ideas based on examples or through visual supports, such as videos and images. This technique also works by passing one or more participants in front to experience an example or exercise.

It consists of the execution of what is exposed. Additional equipment and instruments are usually needed.

The steps to apply it are as follows:

- A general explanation is given, a implementation is carried out by the instructor.

- The explanation is repeated.

- The practice is repeated more slowly.

- It concludes with the realization of the activities in charge of the participants.

Advantages:

- It is necessary to appreciate "in slow motion" the sequence of a process, the manipulation of an apparatus, etc..

- The necessary resources are available.

- For the first time you will handle an instrument, make a stroke, a problem solving, etc.

D. **Experiential**

The instructor performs a group dynamic or a practical exercise where the participants live the experience and learn quickly.

Group dynamics are known as "business games" because they are fun and engaging for people, and because they are fictional.

Group dynamics have also been called "experiential" because they make you live or feel a real situation. Which is very important because today, more than ever, education becomes formative and ceases to be informative to become experiential knowledge. Group dynamics provide experiences in the form of games or exercises with a minimal structure so that people can get the most out of the experience.

Advantages:

- The dynamics for groups acquire a specific value of fun.

- Not only do they stimulate emotionality and creativity, but they also introduce dynamism and positive tension into groups.

- It implies the fact of dissociating oneself from the serious situation of the moment.

- Achieve a deep identification with the job problems. This identification is impossible to obtain otherwise.

INSTRUCTOR TEACHING

Success in teaching the instructor lies in the optimal management of their skills and in using the appropriate instructional technique according to the topic being taught.

Therefore:

> **"Remember that the best instructor is not the one who knows the most,
> but the one that ensures that the participant learn from the topic."**

EFFECTIVE TRAINING

Purchase this book by...

Either in Kindle or Paperback Format

Dominique Daphnis

Understand your fears, break negative patterns and improve your relationships... include personality tests!
www.amazon.com.mx

CHAPTER 9
STORY
"A NEW BEGINNIG"

After my departure from MakeaTeam I took a well-deserved and necessary vacation.

Upon my return, Oscar Ávila, with whom I had worked at Hipotecaria Nacional invited me to work as a freelance instructor for the consultancy Ned Herrman Group, for a project with Infonavit. The project sought to provide training to participants on the new vision of Infonavit and on a new sustainability project. I had to teach courses in Mexico City, Monterrey, Pachuca and Saltillo.

In addition, my friend Sandra Alegría, with whom I had also worked in the mortgage industry, invited me for a very interesting project with Siemens. Few fonths ago, she opened her consultancy Impulsa and was doing very well. Siemens was about to implement a new project called "Evolution", where there would be no enclosed spaces, no cubicles, no private, but common spaces and areas for all. The project consisted in training to all the staff who were in the Vallejo plant on how the move would be carried out and how they would work in their new facilities applying the open space.

EFFECTIVE TRAINING

For the next few months I was quite busy and I didn't lack work. In my spare time I attended several interviews either as a consultant or as a Training Manager.

During the interviews I realized that my position at MakeaTeam was very well paid and above the market. If I was going to hire myself again in a company I would have to be sure that both economically and quality work worth it.

By December 2010 I went to a meal with my sister Roxana, she had a marketing agency and was the one who "introduce me the idea on my brain" to create my own consultancy. She offered with her people to support me in the creation of the website and the logo.

A few days later I met with my friend Mauricio Gleich, he managed "The Entrepenuer Training Gide", a magazine that offers advertising spaces to training consultancies. Mauricio gave me support and offered me a space for the next three months.

I have to admit that at first I had my reservations and a little fear in opening the consultancy, since I was alone and did not know how it was going be. But after several days of thinking about it I made the decision to do it.

A NEW BEGINNING

The first thing I did was to think of the name. To do this, I had to be clear about the mission, vision and values that my consultancy represented.

It became clear to me that, although I had a good experience in training, I not only wanted to focus my work on it, I could also apply several aspects of the Human Resources area, such as Recruitment, Performance Evaluations, Organizational Climate, Job Descriptions, Strategic Planning and Communication.

I established the mission of: "Offer solutions and development to the human resource" of the companies that were my clients. It was then that I came up with the name of my consultancy: SOLDERH (Solutions and Development in Human Resources).

I established the vision: "To be a model consultancy in the future that offers simple, innovative and high-impact solutions".

Finally, to establish the values I should choose the ones that represented me, as well as the ones that anyone who worked at SOLDERH should have. The values established were: Innovation, Quality, Continuous Improvement, Passion, Motivation, Professionalism and Integration.

Once I had defined the name, the mission, and the values I I contacted my sister. She and her team began working on the logo design. Later in the elaboration of the website and finally in an advertisement.

When the logo, page and advertisement were finished I contacted Mauricio. He recorded the data and posted the announcement in the Business Training Guide.

At the same time I registered the documentation with the Secretariat of Finance and Public Credit. On January 2011, SOLDERH was officially founded.

At the beginning there were few calls to make appointments, so I continued to work on my freelance projects with Infonavit and Siemens.

But after a few months, the two projects were finished. He was going to more and more appointments, but he hadn't closed any sales. I knew how to make proposals, but no one had taught me how to sell. I had to learn with practice, but this was costing me to waste opportunities with prospects.

After five months I began to think that maybe I had been wrong. Little by little I began to learn that in the business of consulting is not only enough to have a good proposal, but it is very important to generate trust. The first sale with a prospect is the most difficult, as they don't know you and don't trust you.

In several appointments I was accompanied by a consultant and now good friend, Ana Elena Espinosa, whom I had met months ago in the Infonavit project. Ana is a very prepared and very patient woman, with extensive knowledge in training and Human Resources.

So in mid-2011 we received our first chance. The company Game Express, dedicated to the realization of video games, needed a course of "The Quality Model of the 5 S". Ana would be the instructor, I would support in all the logistics and follow-up with the client.

The following month we got our second sale. Now with a financial company that grants rural loans to people with limited resources. With Financiamiento Progresemos we taught our first pilot course and it was a success.

Also with the company IQ ZONE we began to work on a Strategic Planning project redefining its mission and objectives, as well as creating job descriptions of the new staff to be hired.

EFFECTIVE TRAINING

With Progresemos Financing, courses began to be implemented in its eight branches and soon I was saturating myself with work.

I realized it was time to start hiring people. One person came in in logistics and two instructors started supporting me in the courses.

By the end of the year we closed the sale of a series of courses with Canon Mexicana on "Telephone Attention".

Thus, despite having a hard and difficult first semester, the second began to be promising. The break-even point between sales and expenses was reached in September and from then on the profits began.

By December 2011 and after the first year of operation, SOLDERH was beginning to take shape in a promising manner. The best was yet to come.

Freelance Period
"Siemens Project"
with Sandra Alegría

Freelance Period
"NFONAVIT Project"
Course in Saltillo

Client:: Game Express
with Ana Elena Espinosa

Course in Cuautla
Client: Progresemos Financing

CHAPTER 10
POST-COURSE ACTIONS

It is useless to teach a course if there is no feedback from it. But who should the instructor give feedback to?

The instructor must report the result of the course to:
- Human resources
- Immediate Boss

At the end of a course it is necessary to have documented the realization of the same. That is why it is essential to have:
- Attendance List
- Evaluation Course
- Training Report

If these three documents are well filled out there will be good feedback from the instructor to the area that organized and administered the training.

Good feedback is always essential to correct, make improvements to the course and have quality training.

EFFECTIVE TRAINING

1. ATTENDANCE LIST

It is a document that serves to register the participants of a course and to prove their attendance at it. An attendance list is an official document and on audit (either internal or external) serves to verify that the course was carried out.

The attendance list is divided into two sections: General Data and Participant Data.

General Data must contain the following:
- Course Name
- Venue or Name of the Meeting Room
- Date
- Instructor Name
- Course Schedule

Participant data must have the participant's full name and signature. Optionally, other data can be requested, such as payroll number, address or area.

The following is an example of a Help List Format:

POST-COURSE ACTIONS

ATTENDANCE LIST

COURSE: **VENUE:**
DATE: **INSTRUCTOR:**
START TIME: **END TIME:**

PARTICIPANTS:

No.	NAME	SIGNATURE
1.		
2.		
3.		
4.		
5.		
6.		
7.		
8.		
9.		
10.		
11.		
12.		
13.		
14.		
15.		
16.		
17.		
18.		
19.		
20.		

2. COURSE EVALUATION

It is a document that serves to measure the results of the course. The evaluations are applied by the participants and are the ones who evaluate the training event. The "Course Assessment" is also an official and useful document during an audit.

At the end of the course it is important to leave at least five minutes for the participant to fill out the assessment calmly. A frequent mistake in the instructor during a course is to go beyond the end time of the course and leave little time for the participant for the evaluation. Normally, the participant will fill out the evaluation quickly and without analyzing objetively the content of it.

The evaluation of the course is divided into three sections: aspects to be evaluated, suggestions and course data.

The "Aspects to Evaluate" is a quantitative section with numerical scales to qualify some aspects of the course, such as:

- Course Functionality
- Learning
- Didactic Material
- Instructor
- Logistics

POST-COURSE ACTIONS

The "Suggestions" is a qualitative section with a series of comments to improve the quality of the course. It is important to at least leave the participant a space so they can write in detail their comments and improvement área of the course.

For the "Course Data" is requested:
- Instructor Name
- Course Name
- Deparment or division in which the participant works
- Date

It is recommended to use an anonymous evaluation so that the participants feel free to evaluate the course without fear of any retaliation.

EFFECTIVE TRAINING

COURSE AND INSTRUCTOR EVALUATION

In order to provide you with the best service and get feedback about of the program and team of instructors, we ask for your qualification for each one of the following points, as well as your comments or suggestions.
SOLDERH, thank you for your participation.

	☺ 5	☺ 4	😐 3	☺ 2	☹ 1	TOTAL
Course Evaluation						
Were your course goals met?						
Were the sequence of themes and order?						
Immediate application to job functions?						
Do you think the duration of the course?						
LEARNING						
Can you relate what you learn to your daily activities?						
Did your knowledge expand with this course to what extent?						
Do you change the view you had about your work?						
Do you consider that the topics addressed will be useful in your work team?						
Is your motivation to attend the courses?						
Didactic Material Evaluation						
¿How is the quality of the material?						
Is the vocabulary of the material easy to understand?						
Is the material easy to consult and follow up?						
Was the additional support material used?						
INSTRUCTOR						
Was the instructor's presentation on the subject?						
Did the instructor solve your doubts about the topics presented?						
Was the instructor's handling with the group?						
How do you consider the instructor's mastery of knowledge?						
Was the instructor's punctuality?						
COORDINATION OF LOGISTICS (face-to-face courses only)						
Were the objectives of the Programme set?						
Was the presentation of the topics logical and appropriate?						
Were the schedule, schedule and break?						
The facilities where the event took place?						
Were the food, coffee, soft drinks, pastries?						

Comments and Suggestions _____

Instructor:_____ Department _____

Course Name _____ Date _____

POST-COURSE ACTIONS

3. TRAINNING REPORT

It is a document that it is used to measure the results of the group and its performance during a course. Before filling out a report it is very important to be clear about the objective of it. This is to document the instructor's comments on everything that happened during the course to serve as a reference for future courses. This report is made by the instructor who taught the course.

A training report contains the following structure:
- General Data
- Perception of the Group Instructor
- Logistics and Material Aspects
- Internal Aspects to Consider
- Group Attitude
- Most Notable Participants
- Difficult Participants
- Incidents or Unforeseen Events
- Instructor Feedback

Below is a report format:

EFFECTIVE TRAINING

 SOLDERH

Name of the Course
Qualitative Training Report
Noviember

Date:	yyyy/mmmmmm/dd
Instructor:	Nombre and Surname
Venue:	Place where the course was held.
No. of Attendees summoned:	
No. of Attendees received:	

1.- Perception of the instructors regarding the Group Process: (The general behavior of the attendees, development of the course, reflected attitudes)	
2.- Relevant aspects of Logistics and Material	
3.- Internal aspects to consider for the implementation of the course (ex.- Difficulties faced by participants in putting into practice the knowledge that is reviewed in the program	
4.- General attitude of the group towards the program Excellent, Good, Regular or Bad	
5.- In case of regular or bad, the group indicates that it is necessary to improve: Work tools, Processes, Internal Communication, Policies, Boss attitude, Others (mention which)	
7.- Most outstanding participants	Name and Surname
8.- Less outstanding participants Observed behaviors	Name and Surname
9.- Incidents within the Program	
10.- Instructor Comments (write instructor observations by dynamics)	

POST-COURSE ACTIONS

COURSES   WEBINARS   ABOUT US   BLOG   CONTACT   LOG INN

In Company Courses

We design training programs tailored to your needs to be taught in your facilities or wherever your organization requires it. We create practical solutions taking into account the area and topic to be developed, the academic level and profile of your staff, which allows us to customize our service generating value for the benefit of the goals and development of your staff.

We are at your service in
Sales: 55 4622 7778
ventas@solderh.com

Request a proposal – investment of our Services In Company.

The competences or topics that we offer you to develop to the measures of your needs are:

V	MANAGERIAL SKILLS
V	HUMAN DEVELOPMENT
V	COMMUNICATION
V	CUSTOMER SERVICE
V	SALES
V	HUMAN RESOURCES

EFFECTIVE TRAINING

COURSES   WEBINARS   ABOUT US   BLOG   CONTACT   LOG INN

Trainning

All our courses are based on the methodology of competences and accelerated learning techniques. We ensure that through dynamics, videos and company games; participants easily incorporate new behaviors through playful experiences.

Online Courses

Time Management

With this course you will learn to identify your priorities and make decisions to use your time efficiently.

Adapting to Change in Moments of Crisis

Develop your ability to adapt to the changes and demands of daily work, take advantage of change as an opportunity to achieve the results you want.

Leadership

Learn to apply the different types of leadership depending on the situation.

Negotiation

Become an expert in effective negotiation, develop your skills and make the most of them in the world of work.

Customer Service

Make the service transcend and become a high-value experience that achieves the loyalty of your customers.

Teamwork

Manage to transform your work teams into high performance teams for the fulfillment of the goals in your organization.

CHAPTER 11
STORY
"DEVELOPMENT AND GROWTH"

The growth of SOLDERH occured on 2012. With the entry of logistics personnel and consultants, it was necessary to establish an Operations Manual where the main processes and activities of the logistics process in a consultancy were established in detail. In the next chapter, we will see this process in detail.

It was necessary to establish and document tasks of administration, sales, elaboration of contents, delivery and logistics.

I would be in charge of the administration, sales and content tasks. Due to the number of courses, it was necessary to document and establish processes in the delivery of these.

A "Position Description of the Instructor" and also of the Logistics Coordinator was made. The "Instructor Policies" (by project) and the "Logistics Manual" were established.

As new projects entered, the instructors were given internal training so that they could give quality courses, they were also trained to assemble of reports and diems.

EFFECTIVE TRAINING

The person in charge of logistics was trained to carry out the functions of reproduction of material and assembly of suitcases.

In 2002 we started with a new client and our first convention. It was a company in charge of distributing sterilizer for medical equipment. The convention was in Cancun and was for 30 people. For the event I worked with Oscar Ávila, with whom I had worked at Hipotecaria Nacional and had just left Ned Herman Group. The event consisted of carrying out team building group dynamics and combining basic concepts within the classroom. It was eight hours of hard work, four were outdoors and at middle day with hot temperatures and hard sunlight. At the end, the event was a success and both Oscar and myself, ended up very happy, but very tired.

That year four training modules were sold with Progresemos Financing and by then, to twelve branches office, because this financial institution was growing rapidly. Little by little we were learning more about the operation of microcredits and applying its operation to our courses.

But, without a doubt, the biggest event of 2012 was having close a deal with one of the largest companies of the country. Grupo México is

DEVELOPMENT AND GROWTH

a mining company specialized in obtaining and transforming products such as copper, zinc, gold and silver. Germán Larrea is the owner of Grupo México, whose estimated value is 15 billion dollars. It is a multinational company with several mines and plants in Mexico, Peru and the United States. It has more than 20,000 employees and is listed on the Mexican Stock Exchange.

The contact was made with the Training Subdirector Arelí Fares. Grupo México has very well defined corporate skills and through a TND, its "Corporate Training Calendar" is established annually.

SOLDERH began working on the corporate calendar for the second half of 2012 with the themes of: "Time Management", "Customer Service" and "Negotiation".

Whenever there is a new client I take care of the delivery of the first course to get to know them better, as well as their policies, their work culture and the group environment. Subsequently, I do the Internal Training and delegate it to the other instructors. To teach my first course, I had to travel to Sonora, where Grupo México established their biggest mines. Teaching a course in a mine is a completely new and different experience, but at the same time fascinating. To get to the Cananea mine, I have to take a flight to Hermosillo, three hours approximately. Later, a driver took me in a van for five hours, in which we crossed the state and crossed the mountains. That day is only destinated to travel.

The Training Chief picked me up in his van from the hotel to the training room inside the mine. To enter it there are strict security controls, such as the use of vest, helmet and safety boots. A mining property is a huge complex of several hundred square kilometers and to move from one area to another you have to do it by van. The facilities are prefabricated and single-storey. The rooms are spacious with all services. When I finish the course by the end of the day, a company driver picked me up and we travel to another nearby mining property (usually an hour away) for another course the next day.

There are mines such as "La Caridad", which are located in the mountains, half an hour from Nacozari. There I had to stay inside a "mining colony". A colony is a small town that has prefabricated houses for employees, dining room, school, sports facilities, mini-supermarket and lodging rooms for outsiders (like me). SO, it is a mini-village where employees live.

DEVELOPMENT AND GROWTH

That same year we closed the year teaching courses for Canon. By the end of the year we were seven people working at SOLDERH. That same year we celebrate our first New Year's Eve dinner, where, in addition, gifts were given and a trip was raffled.

On 2013 more courses were involved: with Canon, Progresemos and Grupo México. As we mentioned in chapter 9, the most difficult thing is the first sale, later, when the client already knows our work, the following sales were easier to closed. The key to increased our sales are the reports and results of the courses, since they show more specific areas of opportunity, new improvements are shown and that became in more specific courses. Such as the case of Progresemos Financing on whic of a customer service course, develped on a second part of this course, which covered more specific topics that corrected aspects failed in the first course. Later, more specific ones came out of these courses with topics of "Collection" and "Complaint Management". 2013 was our first year in which we exceeded one million pesos in sales.

The next three years remained good and upward. We retain our previous clients such as Canon, Progresemos and Grupo México. We started working with a logistics company in Queretaro and opened an office in that state. In that period of time, an accountant, four

Instructors and two "Logistics Coordinators" entered SOLDERH. With Progresemos, two modular programs of ten courses each were created, one for branch staff and the other for "Branch Managers" and corporate managers in Mexico. Progresemos grew in five years from eight to twenty-seven branches, and therefore, was an important factor of SOLDERH's growth.

For 2017, work with Progresemos was stopped due to a restructuring in the company. In addition, all the human skills modules had been completed and there was little else to offer. However, that year we worked with two new customers: Assden (manufacturer of auto parts and spare parts for the Metro collective system) and the Infrastructure division of Grupo México, which is responsible for extracting oil, gas and generating electricity (only for self-consumption in the mines and plants of Grupo México).

In 2018, Progresemos recovered with specialized courses for their positions. For this, it was necessary to do research in the field and from there create a manual for, later, the elaboration of the course. We also worked with another new client, Andellac, in the elaboration of a "Strategic Planning Manual" for one of its clients. Likewise, with Grupo México, "Communication" courses were taught, from which several internal campaigns were drawn to improve and promote programs among the communities and the miners.

DEVELOPMENT AND GROWTH

The year 2019 was one in whic were fewer sales and a decrease in relation to previous years. That was why began working on a new business scheme that would encompass having a new partner. Despite not being such a good year, 2019 served as a basis for researching, attracting and generating different course schemes from how they had been given for eight years.

EFFECTIVE TRAINING

DEVELOPMENT AND GROWTH

Our First Year End Dinner
SOLDERH 2012

Team Bulding Integration Event
Grupo México

EFFECTIVE TRAINING

Time Management Course
Client: Assden
in México City

Goals Management Course
Client: CLS
in Querétaro

CHAPTER 12
THE PROTAGONISTS OF THE TRAINNING PROCES

In the past chapters we review what is done before, during and after a course has been taught.

But we have not analyzed the protagonists of this process. In this chapter we will review the training process, both internal and external.

We call it internal when it is the company itself that organizes and teaches the course.

The external is when the company (either due to lack of time or because it does not have the expertise) hires a consultancy to develop and teach the course, in this case, the planning of the same is carried out by both parties.

It should be noted that the process is the same, whether the company is small, medium or large or a multinational corporation. What changes are the functions and activities that the protagonists of the process will have.

1. THE TRAINNING PROCESS IN A COMPANY

Below is a general presentation of the training process in a company:

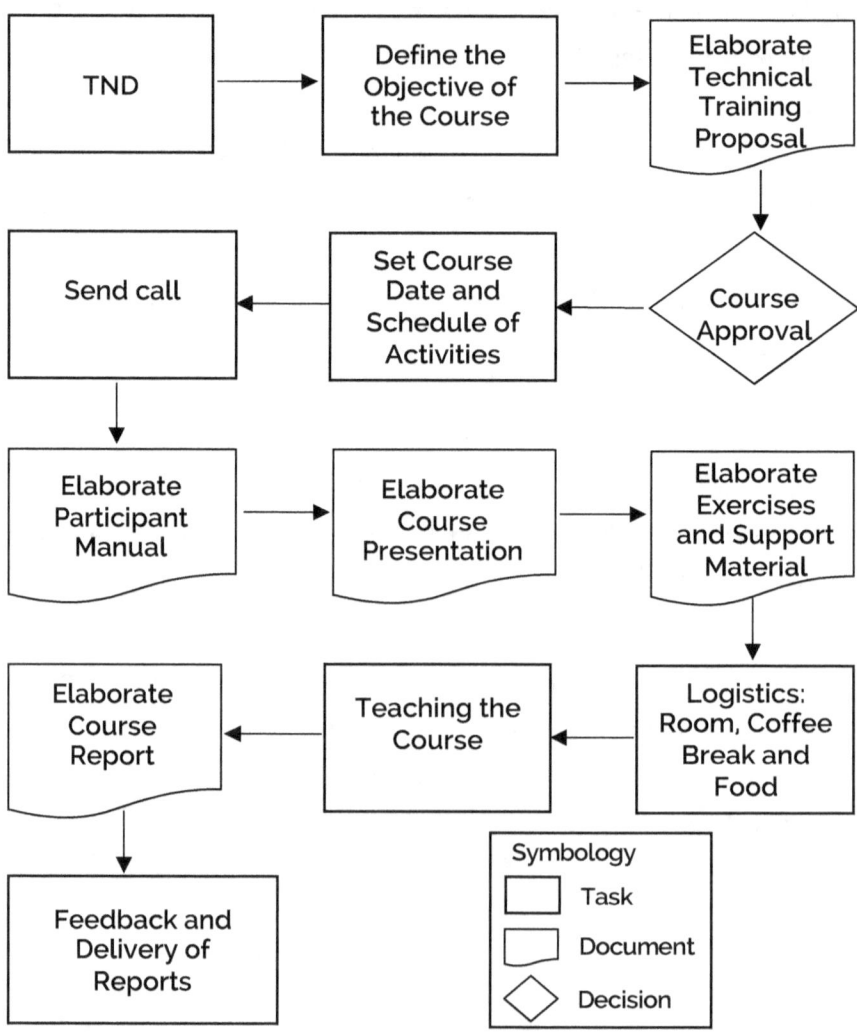

THE PROTAGONISTS OF THE TRAINNING PROCESS

First, the training area designs and applies the Training Needs Diagnosis (TND) to staff. Subsequently, it analyzes the results and determines which courses have to be carried out in a certain period.

The next thing is to determine the general and specific objectives of each course to be taught.

Then, either to the Human Resources Director or General Director (if it is a small company) the Technical Training Proposal (background, objectives, agenda, investment and logistics) is presented.

Once the proposal is submitted, it is decided which courses are approved and which are not.

Immediately after approval, the dates of each course are established. These are confirmed with those responsible for the areas involved and if it is necessary to make changes they are made. Already with the final dates, a schedule of activities is made for each of the courses.

Subsequently, the call is sent via email to inform the participants of the course. The call must indicate the name of the course, the date, time, place, the objectives and the topics. Depending on the company there are mandatory and invitational courses.

Then is the ealaboration of Course Manual, which is desinged in accordance with the provisions of the Technical Training Proposal. The manual is a key document for developing the Course Presentation, which will be more illustrative and summarized compared to the manual. Then the exercises and support materials of the course are made, reproduced and stored in suitcases for transportation to the room.

Days before the sesión, the logistics part is planned, with tasks suchs as the classroom, as well as the coffee break and food. The course can be carried out in company facilities or in a hotel.

The instructor who teaches the course must arrive 30 minutes early to connect their equipment and install their material. Later teaches the course and at the end, collects the surplus material.

After the course, the instructor prepares a report and days later there is a meeting in which the reports are delivered and feedback is given with the results of the course.

THE PROTAGONISTS OF THE TRAINNING PROCESS

Below we will see the protagonists of this process, the activities and the documents they carry out.

A. Trainning Manager

Is responsible for the area. Works in medium, large and multinational corporate companies. Reports to the Director of Human Resources. Within the process it is responsible for:

- Design the TND questionnaire.
- Establish the objectives of the course.
- Prepare and present the Technical Training Proposal
- Set date.
- Receive course feedback from the instructor.
- Verify that all process activities are successful.

In addition, carries out other tasks such as:

- Budget of the area.
- Review with the Head of Human Resources, the training programs that will be carried out in the year.
- Has meetings with other areas of the company to offer them the internal and external courses that are needed.

- Meetings with trainning team to carry out the established courses.
- Evaluate the performance of your team in charge.
- Approves training proposals from external consultancies.

B. Trainning Instructor

Is responsible for delivering the training courses. Can appear in any size of company. In a small company it reports to the head of Human Resources, in medium or large companies to the Training Manager. In a small company carries out all the activities of the process. In a medium or large company is responsible for:

- Prepare the manual and presentation of the course.
- Develop exercises and support material.
- Teaching of courses.
- Prepare training reports.
- Course feedback.

Also carries out other tasks like:

- Attend meetings with the Training Manager and the entire team to review the area's weekly activities.

THE PROTAGONISTS OF THE TRAINNING PROCESS

- Research and learn from the internal activities and processes of other areas to take new courses.
- Trains and feeds back the training team from operation and other areas of the company.

C. Trainning Analist

Is responsible for carrying out all the analytical, statistical and numerical information of the training. This position usually only exists in large companies. Reports to the Training Manager. Within the training process is responsible for:

- Apply the TND.
- Encode TND results.
- Develop the schedule activities of a course.

Also carries out other tasks, such as:
- Preparation of reports of training programs.
- Preparation of Expense Reports of the area.
- Grade exams (if applied in courses).
- Attend meetings with the Training Manager and the entire team to review the area's weekly activities.

D. **Trainning Coordinator or Trainning Assistant**

Is responsible for executing logistics activities. This position usually only exists in medium and large companies. Reports to the Training Manager. Within the training process is responsible for:

- Send the call for courses.
- Print and assemble the support material of a course.
- Preparation of the room, food and coffee break.

Also carries out other tasks, such as:

- Print the TND questionnaires.
- Apply the questionnaires (if there is no analyst).
- Preparation and printing of diplomas or certificates.
- Take calls from the area.
- Research and take budgets.
- Safeguarding and archiving of training material:
    - Manuals and Presentations.
    - Attendance Lists and Reports.
    - Evaluations and Exams.
    - Expense Invoices.
- Attend meetings with the Training Manager and the entire team to review area activities.

2. THE TRAINNING PROCESS IN A CONSULTANCY

Below is a general presentation of the training process in a company:

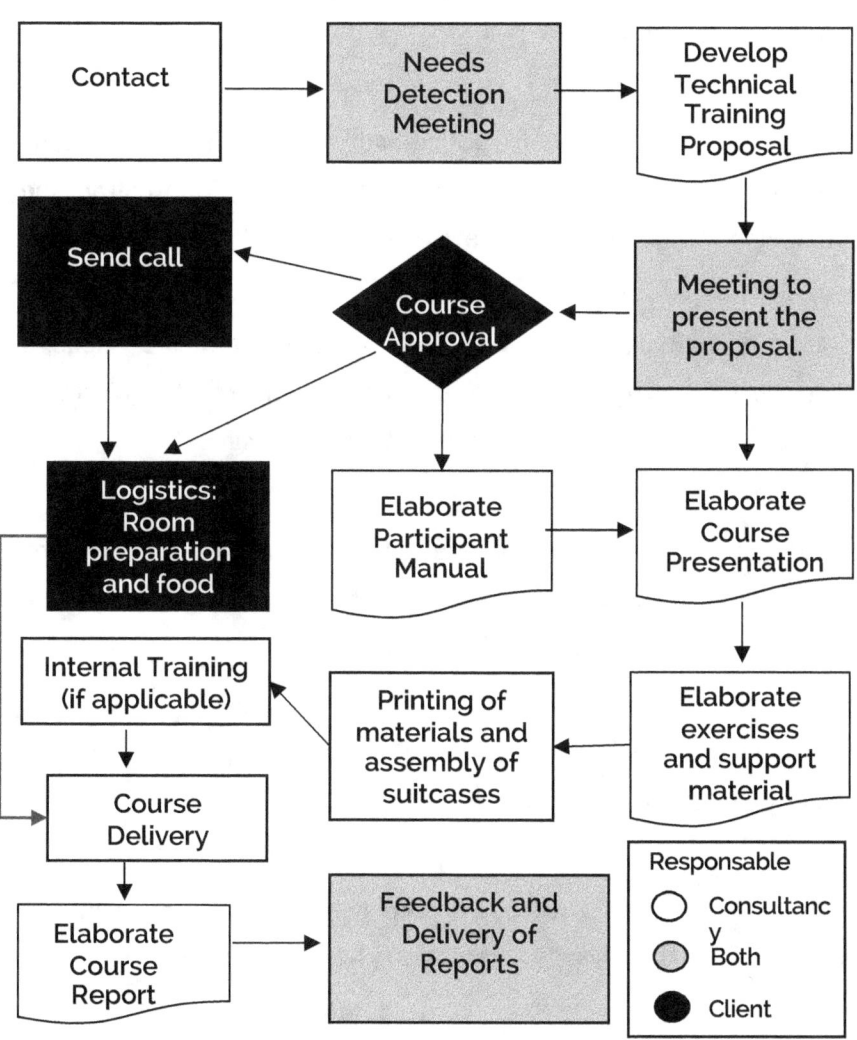

First is the contact with the prospect or client. Prospect when never has been worked with it and client if there have already worked previously. This contact is made through a phone call and an scheduled an appointment.

During the meeting, the background and problems that the company has are analyzed and needs are detected to determine what are the competencies that have to be developed.

With the information gathered during the meeting to detect needs, a Technical Training Proposal is made (background, objectives, methodology, agenda, general conditions and investment).

Then is a second meeting with the client or prospect and the finished proposal is presented. If there are changes or corrections, the proposal is adjusted again until it is finished.

Subsequently, the course is approved, the proposal is signed, as well as a contract or service order.

Once the course is approved, the client is responsible for sending the call as well as the logistics regarding the headquarters and food.

THE PROTAGONISTS OF THE TRAINNING PROCESS

Meanwhile, the consultancy is responsible for preparing the Participant Manual in accordance with the provisions of the Technical Training Proposal.

The manual prepares the presentation of the course and later, the exercises and the support material.

Then all the materials are printed and suitcases are assembled for transportation to the course venue.

If the course is going to be given by several instructors, an "Internal Training" is done. There is a course training session in order to train instructors on show how they should deliver the course.

Later the course is developed. For this it is recommended that the instructor arrives 30 minutes before the session to connect his equipment. Later teaches the course and at the end collects the surplus material.

After the course, the instructor prepares a report and days later there is a meeting in which the reports are delivered and feedback is given with the results of the course

Below we will see the protagonists of this process, the activities and the documents they carry out.

A. Consultant

The consultant work is very complete, and is a specialist in:

- Needs detection.
- Content development.
- Logistics.
- Course delivery.
- Feedback.

In small consultancies, is in charge of doing all the activities of the process. In a large consultancy specializes in the development of content and delivery of courses.

The consultant must have a great adaptability to adjust to different ways of working with each client. Also must read constantly and update on new training topics.

B. Sales Manager

The job is to sell courses and attract new customers. In a large consultancy reports the director of the consultancy.

THE PROTAGONISTS OF THE TRAINNING PROCESS

Within the process it is responsible for:
- Contact with the prospect or client.
- Meeting to detect needs.
- Develop Technical Training Proposal.
- Meeting to present the proposal.
- Teaching courses (does so sporadically).
- Feedback and delivery of reports with the client.

Also carries out other tasks, such as:
- Prospecting.
- Signing of proposals and contracts.
- Meeting with the Content Manager to land the proposal to a content.
- Make a summary of all the courses in a period to provide feedback to the client.
- Prepare Sales Report.

C. Content Manager

The job is to create the contents of the courses. In a large consultancy can have a group of consultants to report to the position and help to generate the contents. Reports to the Director of the Consultancy. Within the process it is responsible for:

- Preparation of Participant Manuals.
- Preparation of course presentations.
- Preparation of exercises and support material.
- Teaching courses (does so sporadically).
- Is in charge of carrying out the Internal Training.

Also carries out other tasks, such as:

- Read and research either books, articles on the internet or magazines.
- Accompany the Sales Manager to meetings with clients.
- Elaboration and testing of group dynamics.
- Elaboration of "Checklist of Materials" for a course.
- Meeting with the Sales Manager and consultants to measure the effectiveness of the contents.

D. Freelance Instructor

Is a specialist in the delivery of courses. The freelancer is external to the consultancy. He is not on the payroll and is paid per course taught. Reports to the "Project Leader", usually (Sales Manager). Within the process it is responsible for:

THE PROTAGONISTS OF THE TRAINNING PROCESS

- Receive internal training.
- Teaching Courses.
- Preparation of Reports.

Also carries out other activities, such as:
- Preparation of Travel Report (if the course was in another city).
- Meeting with the Sales Manager for feedback on the courses he taught.

D. Logístics Coordinator

Is responsible for coordinating all the courses that have been contracted. In a large consultancy reports to the Content Manager. Within the process is responsible for:
- Printing of materials and assembly of suitcases.

Also carries out other tasks such as:
- Send the course schedule to consultants.
- Send invitation courses to freelance instructors.
- Hotel reservations.
- Buy airline tickets.

- Purchase of materials and supplies for the courses of the period.
- Receipt of delivery of material after a course.
- Review of per diem reports.

E. **Director**

Is responsible for the results of the consultancy. Is reported by the Sales Manager and the Content Manager. Is responsible for supervising all the activities of the process. A Director should have been a consultant in the beginning.

Also carries out other tasks, such as:
- Establishment of objectives and goals.
- Preparation of the Business Plan (annual).
- Revenue Projection.
- Expense Budget.
- Supervision and payment to internal and external staff.
- Payment to suppliers.
- Supervise the Sales Manager for the collection of invoices.
- Create and plan new business schemes.

THE PROTAGONISTS OF THE TRAINNING PROCESS

EFFECTIVE TRAINING

In Hunter Asesores we are specialists in the definition of the central campaign message, based on semiotic guidelines that reach people's emotions.

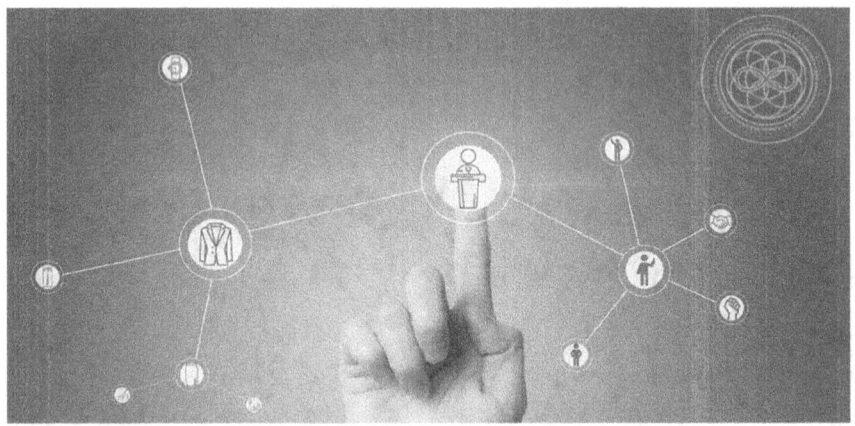

We offer services for:
- Political Campaigns
- Governments
- Political parties

www.hunterasesores.com

CHAPTER 13
STORY
"EVOLVING INTO A NEW FUTURE"

The year 2019 was a complicated one because analyzing the situation I realized that I had to evolve in the business scheme.

For eight years, SOLDERH had specialized in teaching courses to companies, we had never done it to individuals. Several years I analyzed the possibility of teaching open courses (to individuals). However, all the complications of logistics and lack of time made me give up on that idea.

In that year, the market and circumstances were no longer the same. That's why I decided to open this new business scheme. However, this I couldn't do alone or with the staff I had. I needed a visionary person, marketing expert and a team expert in communication and design. That's how I partnered with the company Hunter Asesores, which would help me create and land this training scheme of courses at the individual level.

As a first step, the website had to be updated, which was already obsolete and had not been maintained for eight years. It was changed platform and reassembled with the previous menus.

Later and to refresh the page it was decided to make some faint modifications to the logo. The olive green tone was changed to the flag green and the above and bottom lines of the logo were stylized.

Before the makeover, there were already sections of: About Us, Courses, Other Services, Customers and Contact.

Before starting to make changes to the page, a Market Study and a first Competitor Analysis were made. Hunter Asesores was in charge of doing the Market Research and seeing the preferences of the people who took courses individually. I, was in charge of analyzing pages of other consultancies and seeing what they offered. These studies helped me to clarify my mind, to take new ideas and apply what I needed.

From the results of these two studies the decision was made with the new business scheme to add the section of: Blog and Photos of the courses. Blogs are articles that talk about a topic related to the courses being offered.

The Courses section was subdivided into two sections: "In Company Courses" (to companies) and "Open" (to people). The "In Company Courses" section shows the competencies that can be developed to offer a client the type of course of thier needs.

The "Open Courses" section had a graphic list of courses and in each one, when clicked, the objectives, the syllabus and the competences to be developed appeared.

However, the most important change had not occurred: it was necessary to convert the page into an "Online Store" to ensure the payment of a course in advance. One of the main problems is that unfortunately in Mexico things are left at the last minute and canceled. For individual courses it is no exception. First, SOLDERH must invest in one room and coffee break and food services, so you can't risk fifteen people signing up for a course and only three attending. That is why this store system ensures the payment in advance of the people who register. To convert SOLDERH into a store we use the "PayPal" payment system or payment via electronic transfer. In case the number of participants is less than the minimum to recover the investment, your money is returned to the registered person.

Once the website was completed, a SOLDERH page was made on Facebook and another on LinkedIn. Both were made with a mechanic similar to the main page on the internet and both have a link to the online store.

EFFECTIVE TRAINING

So, in 2020 we were ready to teach our first open course when the Covid-19 contingency reached us. That stopped our entire operation and the course had to be postponed. As the weeks passed, seeing that the situation was not improving and realizing the number of webinars that were taking place, it was decided to create another new business scheme in conjunction with Hunter Asesores.

It was thus decided to create the division of online courses. To do this, the first thing we did was to do a market study again. The study determined that the public that buys online courses is different from the one that attends a cuourse in person. He is younger, people has different interests and different economic income.

As a result of the research, it was necessary to make a restructuring and change of image that would adapt to the three types of clients that SOLDERH had from now on: for in-company courses, aimed at companies with a high budget; for the Open Courses, focused on middle-aged middle-aged people (middle- and upper-income), and finally, for the Online Courses, focused on middle- and low-income young people.

This is how work was first done to determine solderh's "brand identity". To define this brand identity, a "Semiotic Study" is made with archetypes. The archetype is the image symbolic that refers to emotional or behavioral patterns that remain engraved in the unconscious. A relationship was made between the personality of the brand and the three types of audience to which SOLDERH is addressed, and from there the Symbolic Figure of the brand was constituted, giving final step to the Personality of the Brand. In this, the colors that the logo must have and everything related to its image are defined. Subsequently, through the process of "Route of Significance", the "Brand Identity" is generated.

Already with a Brand Identity a sketch of the logo was made and then its acceptance was tested in a Focus Group (diverse group of people who express their visual impressions of the logo). Corrections are then made to the logo and re-evaluated in another Focus Group. This process is repeated several times until the final logo remains.

With the finished logo, a "Graphic Identity Manual" is made. This manual indicates all the permitted and non-permitted uses that can be given to the logo and its colors, how to apply them on letterheads, presentations, manuals, videos, web pages and business cards.

From there all new image is applied to all electronic files, physical documents, courses, email and Internet pages.

With the new image ready, another Competitor Analysis was made, but this one was now focused only on companies that offer online courses. During this analysis, strengths and areas of improvement of each page that was analyzed were observed. It was determined that there are currently several ways to upload online courses of different qualities. The best ideas were taken, the structure, the way to carry it out, the duration and the cost of them were determined. Few Human Resources consultancies offer online courses.

SOLDERH, in most of its courses, uses the methodology of accelerated learning through group dynamics. However, implementing this methodology in online courses involves a challenge. Finally, by making many adjustments to group dynamics, with many hours of work and tests, this could become a reality.

Currently, SOLDERH is the first Mexican consultancy in Human Resources with accelerated learning methodology to offer the three training schemes: In Company Courses, Open Courses and Online Courses.

EVOLVING INTO A NEW FUTURE

SOLDERH Initial Logo

Online Store
Open Course: Adaptability to Change in Times of Crisis

EFFECTIVE TRAINING

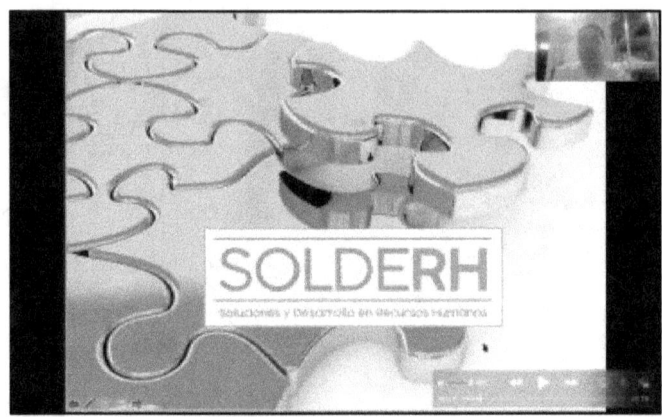

First Online Course
Pilot Course
SOLDERH 2020

SOLDERH
Current Logo

CHAPTER 14
E-LEARNING

In the previous chapters we review in detail the entire process of face-to-face training, what is done before, during and after a course. We also saw how training is organized and executed, both from within a company and from outside through an external consultancy. Finally, we saw the functions that each of the training positions have, both in a company and in a consultancy.

Now, in this last chapter, we will address the topic of distance learning, its definition, its history, the benefits it offers, its limitations, online courses for both companies and individuals, to culminate with the design and the way of teaching.

We can define distance learning as:

"The training that is carried out virtually through a tool, where the participant is in a different place from the instructor."

Normally, the tool that communicates to the instructor is a computer with special software to be able to carry out a training.

1. HISTORY

The history of distance learning is closely linked to the development of technology. One might think that you can only give remote training with a computer, but it wasn't always this way.

A. Correspondence Teaching

It began in the nineteenth century in Britain, where courses in trades were given by correspondence. In the late nineteenth and early twentieth centuries it began to be incorporated into some universities in the United States, such as Chicago and Calvert, in Baltimore. By 1930 there were already 39 universities offering distance courses.

B. Multimedia Teaching

Its peak was during the decades of the 60s and 70s. It emerged in 1960 from the British Open University. The instructor appears, who acts as a mediator between the participant and the teaching material. During this stage, means of communication such as telephone, television, radio, audiocasettes and videocasettes were used. During this stage, at the teaching level, Distance Education began to be developed around the world in universities.

E-LEARNING

C. Telematics Teaching

The use of information and communication technologies applies. In 1970 the use of the computer was integrated. In 1980 telecommunications were integrated and videoconferencing and interactive distance learning emerged, where the instructor and participants communicated live. Courses were given assisted with the CD-ROM. In 1989 the World Wide Web (www) internet was born. The first computer courses began to be given directly.

B. Virtuales Learning Environments

It occured in the 90s with the expansion of the internet and e-learning as we know today. Virtual groups are created where the instructor and each participant meet in different places. In 1994 virtual universities emerged. As the years go by, better software is used to teach courses, either recorded or live and with high resolution image quality. Initially, programs to transmit e-learning were limited and expensive. Currently there are pages that offer services at very affordable costs and with good image quality. In addition, now, the platforms allow you to prepare exams and display personalized recognitions at the end of a session.

2. BENEFITS

Overall, people are busier and technology made massive advances, so online learning is becoming a much more attractive option when it comes to personal and professional development.

- **Profitability**

    With online training, the employees can access courses anywhere, providing convenience and saving money. Another advantage is probable to find reduced prices when forming large groups of employees, which will allow greater savings. With online courses you can save costs for transfers.

- **Time**

    Online courses, in addition to money, save participants time, becuase people do not have to move from their workplace to the classroom. In addition, online courses are generally shorter in time. An e-learning course session that lasts more than two hours continuous becomes tiring and tedious.

- **Consistency**

    No matter how many employees you have, online training courses provide the same content for everyone.

- **Variability**

    Not all employees will need the same training at the same time. Investing in online training gives the opportunity and flexibility to specially tailor each employee's professional development. It also helps staff retention, as employees will be happy that time, money, and interest is being invested in their training.

- **Immediacy**

    After completing an online course, employees will receive immediate results and feedback on their performance. Users can also track their progress and review areas of misunderstanding before completing the assessment. In addition, most online training courses provide a certificate of completion.

- **Supporting Content**

    Interactive online courses will provide your learners with active learning, helping them increase retention of course material. Online courses are supported by audiovisual materials such as video, which facilitates learning through the senses.

3. LIMITATIONS

Just as it has its benefits, distance learning has its limitations. Some of them are:

- **Incompatible for certain courses**

    Not all courses are useful through distance communication. The development of human skills requires practice. For example, it is not useful to learn a driving course by e-learning. It is best to take face-to-face classes and practice driving with an instructor.

- **Impersonal**

    Receiving an education in a traditional class is an activity that happens within a social context. Interacting with other people is not central to an Online Course. Some people absolutely need an instructor to learn a new subject.

- **Learn from a computer screen**

    Learning from a computer for hours, without breaks, can cause decreased vision, tiredness injuries, and back problems. In addition, some topics require practice and cannot be taught simply with online lessons.

- **A lot os discipline is required**

    If participants do not have self-discipline it is very unlikely that they will be motivated to complete their Online Courses. There is no one to tell them that they have to sit down and start their studies.

In conclusion, Online Courses are a novelty in the educational world. But are they going to replace traditional education? No. Online Courses are not made for all people or studies. However, Online Courses are very effective for informational type training, induction courses or very specific courses. Traditional education will exist anyway, but online education will become more and more present in our daily lives.

4. IN COMPANY ONLINE COURSES

As we saw before, in-company courses are those that are aimed at closed groups within a company.

Every day more companies are investing in e-learning courses. It all depends on the size of the company, your training needs, and your budget.

Currently there are a large number of platforms and specialized websites to provide the service for each company needs.

Below we will see some platforms and internet pages that are used to give In Company Courses online:

- **SAP**

    It is one of the most complete business platforms for companies in the world. It serves to automate processes and in the different areas of a company. If the company wishes, the SAP provider generates an e-learning module for the company. The cost of this platform is very high, it is usually used by multinational corporations. The e-learning module is one of the many offered by this platform.

- **Moodle**

    It is one of the most widespread platforms worldwide, being the option chosen by the largest number of universities. It offers a large number of functionalities and possibilities. Its cost depends on the needs of the project and the number of options that are configured for it. It can be used both for the e-learning modality and to complement face-to-face learning.

- **Chamilo**

    It is an LMS (Learning Method Sistem) fork of Dokeos, which includes social functions (chat, messaging and workgroups) more efficiently and easily than Moodle. The technical demands are also lower and both its learning curve and its interface are friendlier. It makes better use of graphic elements, using icons that make the user experience more intuitive. It has a high cost, but more accessible than the previous two.

- **WordPress**

    WordPress, the CMS with which 26% of the world's websites are made and which supports 30% of e-commerce, has developed in recent years LMS solutions of high quality. It provides a total adaptation and transparency with the corporate image, since it never leaves the website. Maintenance can even be easily carried out by the organization's staff, with much less expensive training and a much faster learning curve. Its cost is medium to high and functional for medium and large companies.

- **Hotmart**

    It is a page that offers space for sale of products online.

It is a page that has a very low cost and is functional for small companies with less than 50 employees. The advantage of this page is that it is paid monthly and there are several plans that are increasing according to the number of courses and participants. It is not very easy to use although it is very interactive.

- **Zoom**

   It is a simple application that serves to hold meetings. It can be used to provide simple distance training within companies. Its main limitation is that it does not have measurement systems such as exams nor can files be downloaded. It only works for live course training. A monthly payment is paid at a low cost. Small and medium-sized businesses can be useful.

- **Webex**

   Like Zoom, it is an application that serves to carry out meetings. It can be used to provide distance training within companies. It also does not have measurement systems nor can files be downloaded. It is limited to the quality of internet bandwidth. It only works for live course training. Monthly payments are paid at low cost. It is useful in medium and small companies.

5. OPEN ONLINE COURSES

As we saw before, open courses are those that are aimed at anyone who wants to receive training.

Every day there are more people who dedicate their time to take Open Online Courses. There are currently a large number of online courses, as well as a wide variety of pages offering them. The most common are:

- **Udemy**

    It is one of the main online courses pages in the world. It is characterized by the great variety of courses it offers. The costs are generally quite affordable. It has a scheme similar to that of UBER (software for the taxi service), since it offers the instructor to promote his course on the page in exchange for him designing the course and teaching it, both parties share 50% of the sales for each course. The quality of the courses is very variable, since it depends on the design and the teaching ability that each instructor has. The main attribute is that almost any course can be found at low cost.

- **Domestika**

    It is a page specialized in courses in design, photography, sales and marketing. The cost per course is medium, but the quality of its contents is high. It is an interactive page that handles didactic and practical courses. It lacks more topics and options for the Human Development part.

- **Yeira**

    It is a simple page that offers good quality courses. Costs are affordable, but more variety is lacking on topics.

- **GoConqr**

    Platform that offers space to design e-learning courses, exams and exercises. It is more focused on the student part than on the professional part. It has a network of users like Facebook. On this page you can create courses, mind mappping, notes, assessments, diagrams. It is not inexpensive, although its use is more for student and academic purposes. The design of the page is attractive and easy to use.

6. DESIGN AND TEACHING

It is recommended to use the online training system for informative courses, relating to a position, policies or procedures. It is not recommended to use online courses to develop human skills, that's what face-to-face courses are for..

E-LEARNING

Unlike face-to-face courses, distance learning goes through the two stages: Preparation and Online Participation.

A. **Preparation**

If the course is In company it is necessary to first make a DNC and then a technical training proposal, once it is approved. It is recommended that an online course should not last more than two hours.

a) **Live**

If the course is live, a manual is made so that it can be downloaded by the participant and a presentation is made that will serve as support material. If the course has videos, it is recommended that they be linked to the presentation. As the course is virtual, the electronic supports must be uploaded to the platform you have so that the participant can use them. It is recommended to apply an exam, either at the end of each module or at the end of the course.

To apply all of the above, you have to master the use of the page or platform on which you are working. If not, the support of a technical support person, systems or the tool provider is necessary.

b. Recorded

If the course is recorded, a manual is also made so that it can be downloaded by the participant and a presentation is made, which will serve as support material. However, the work is more complex, since they must be recorded with a camera, both to the instructor and the presentation which is explained at the moment. As a movie of a course, It es necessary to record the modules separately and if there are errors or failures, it is necessary to edit the recorded video. At the end, the course will be composed of the recorded modules. It is recommended that each recorded module does not exceed 10 minutes. If videos are presented, they must be linked to the presentation. Electronic supports must be uploaded to the platform. It is recommended to apply an assessment to measure learning.

To apply all this you have to master the use of the page or platform, frame well in camera and know how to handle a video editing program. If the the course material is of high quality, the support of specialized multimedia personnel will be necessary for recording and editing.

E-LEARNING

B. Online Participation

If the course is In Company, taking it may be optional or may be mandatory. Within a company, if the course is mandatory, the call to it establishes a deadline to take it. If the course is open, the participant registers, fills out a form and pays online (there are also free courses).

a) Live

If the course is live, the participant receives an invitation with a link to access the session and enter the course. Normally, during the session, the instructor asks the group to have the microphones disconnected from their computers while giving their explanations, to prevent any sound from entering that interrupts or distracts everyone. The question and answer sessions can be given by chat or at the end of each module, where the instructor gives the instruction to the participants to open their microphones. The advantage of this type of session is that a large number of people can enter at the same time. The main disadvantage is that it is difficult to answer all the questions. Short sessions that take place live and do not exceed the time are called webinars. At the end of the session an exam can be applied through the platform and the system downloads the personalized recognition of the participant.

b) Recorded

If the course is recorded, the participant enters the system or page and enters the course. It will give you to play each of the modules or if the course does not have video, it will read the texts of each module. There are courses whose videos are linked to YouTube and the page gives access through a link. The advantage of this type of training is that if the participant was distracted or did not understand a concept, they can pause the video, return it and repeat the explanation. A recorded course has the advantage that it can be taken at any time and anywhere. At the end of the session an exam can be applied through the platform and the system downloads the personalized certificate of the participant.

E-LEARNING

COURSES   WEBINARS   ABOUT US   BLOG   CONTACT   LOG INN

Services

Integration & Team Building

Wide variety of outdoor dynamics for events and conventions. Expert consultants in mass events ranging from 50 to 2000 people. These dynamics promote teamwork and the integration of people.

Personnel Recruitment

We have a team of specialized and trained recruiters that will help you select the staff according to the profile you need for your company.

Organizational Environment

We elaborate, manage and deliver an analysis of the work environment, through a qualitative and quantitative survey.

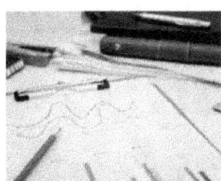

360 Performance Evaluations

We offer solutions to improve the performance of your employees, through an evaluation that aligns the job description with the mission and objectives of the company.

Strategic Pleaning

We support you to define what is the mission, visison and institutional values of your organization. We help you establish the main objectives of the organization, as well as the tactical and operational planning to land the objectives in strategies and actions to middle and operational managers of your company.

Job Description

We help you define the competencies required to design the job descriptions your company needs.

EFFECTIVE TRAINING

   COURSES   WEBINARS   ABOUT US   BLOG   CONTACT   LOG INN

Contact

We have 2 offices:

SOLDERH QUERÉTARO
Via Catania 18 int 35. Col. Villa Catania. El Marqués, Qro. C.P. 76246

SOLDERH MEXICO CITY
Alfonso Caso Andrade 48 -6. Col. Las Águilas Ciudad de México C.P. 01710

Phones:

+52 (442) 455 2612

+52 (55) 4622 7778

Schedules:

Monday to Friday from 9:00 am to 6:00 pm

Contact us on Facebook

Your Name (required)

Your Email (required)

Matter

Message

SEND

CONCLUSIONS

This book is a reflection of my work in the area of training for more than 20 years. This work was divided into two parts. The nones chapters dealt with my entire career, experiences, satisfactions, sufferings, problems, learning, reflections, changes and much more. The even chapters narrate what I consider to be the proper way to work to teach a course, what is done to get it approved, the whole planning process, the teaching and what is reported after a course has been given.

This book is intended for all who have given or received training. To those who have taught courses so that they can take into account all the details involved in doing a course and can perfect it. Remember that if you work in this medium, you always have to be open to learning and our work is always perfectible and improvable.

Below I present a series of recommendations so that you can apply what is seen in this book through concrete actions:

1. Be very clear about the objective of the course you are going to teach and correctly elaborate a Technical Training Proposal.

2. Prepare manuals and training presentations appropriate to the course you are going to teach.

EFFECTIVE TRAINING

3. When teaching, pay attention, observe the group, listen to the participants and have a lot of patience with them.

4. Make an analysis of what they are asking you and give clear and simple explanations so that the participant understands you.

5. Teach your courses mastering the exhibition technique and complement your exhibition using interrogative, demonstrative and if possible experiential elements.

6. Prepare correctly and deliver your training reports to the corresponding area on the required date.

7. Uses online courses to disseminate technical or informational content; you don't want to develop human skills online, it's not the right way.

8. Decide if your online course will be live or recorded, and discuss what the benefits of that decision you made are.

9. If your online course is live, you should check that all the auxiliaries of your transmission work correctly, such as the internet, microphones, camera verify any external sounds are not spoiling your transmission.

10. If your course is recorded you must subdivide it into modules and lessons that do not exceed 10 minutes, each. Each recording should be technically perfect, if there are errors, you will need to edit the video.

CONCLUSIONS

If you are one of those who receive training constantly, either within your company or voluntarily attend open courses on your own or take them online, this book will be useful to you. You have understood that a good course is not only about the oratory skills that the instructor has, but that it must have extensive preparation and planning, as well as actions of how the course can be applied on a day-to-day basis.

A course, no matter how fun and interesting its topic, if it is not applicable to your work or personal life, is a course that does not work. Whether it's the company where you work or yourself, you will have wasted your time, your money and your effort.

Here are some recommendations so you can apply what you have seen in a course:

1. Always analyze the objective and syllabus of the course, if it is applicable to your work or personal life.

2. You should receive a support material, either a manual, the presentation or a workbook that serves as a guide. If an instructor doesn't give you support material, they're not being professional.

3. When you attend the session try to arrive rested because you will require a lot of energy to listen and learn.

4. Listen, analyze and take note of the information you consider relevant during the session.

5. Whenever you have any doubt, question, there is no worse question than the one that is not asked. Do not feel sorry to ask, you are there to learn and the instructor is at your service to guide and support you.

6. Collaborate and participate, but do not try to be the protagonist of the session. Let others participate and contribute to the group.

7. When you do the course assessment, be objective. Don't evaluate the instructor low if you liked him badly or high if you liked him; make an objective assessment based on the usefulness of the course and areas for improvement. Write down your comments at the end of the evaluation.

8. If your course is online, analyze the objective of the course and whether it is applicable to what you are looking for.

9. If the online course is live, be punctual because the sessions are short and the minutes you miss will no longer be able to replenish them.

10. If the course is recorded and you did not understand some concept, you have the advantage of pausing the video and returning it to listen again to the part that you did not understand.

Finally, whether you are a trainer or a participant, always have the availability and vocation to learn. In a course everyone learns, both the participants learn from the instructor, and the instructor of the participants.

ACKNOWLEDGMENTS

To my friend Jean Dominique Daphnis, for supporting and guiding me throughout the process of publishing this book.

To José Luis Arizaleta for his friendship, support and for the realization of the Prologue of this book.

To Enrique and Alicia Enciso for giving me the opportunity to work at Barter and have my first experience in the field of training.

To Jaqueline Flores for the team we formed and everything we were able to land in Barter.

To Bárbara Chaparro for believing in me and helping me develop my potential.

To Adalberto Samaia for being my first teacher, to whom I learned that creativity, learning and fun can be together and be very effective.

To Gloria Gómez Palacio for her trust, for her patience and for giving me the freedom to learn from other areas of Hipotecaria Nacional.

To Luis Farías, Mariana Ríos, Octavio Coronado, Gaby León and Pablo Zolle, for being the best consultants I have ever worked with and for everything I learned from each of you.

To Oscar Ávila, for inviting me to work on the INFONAVIT project and its teachings during my stay at Hipotecaria Nacional.

To Sandra Alegría for her friendship and for inviting me to work on the innovative Siemens project.

To Mauricio Gleich, for his friendship and for his support in opening a space for SOLDERH in the Business Training Guide.

To my sister Roxana, for helping me develop SOLDERH.

To Alfonso Velázquez and Carlos Martínez for their loyalty and effort during the years they have worked at SOLDERH.

Finally to you, for giving you the time and space to read this book, to make the most of what you learned from this work. Don't make the mistakes I made, take the opportunities that come your way and whatever you do, do it with passion.

BIBLIOGRAPHY

El ABC de la Capacitación, Maxwell John, Vergara y Riba, 2007

Capacitación y Desarrollo de Personal, Grados Espinos Jaime, Trillas, 2009

Aprender Jugando: Dinámicas Vivenciales para la Capacitación y Docencia, Acevedo, Alejandro, Limusa, 2008

Aprendiendo a Aprender, Novak, Jay, Martínez Roca, 2002

El Método Obama, Swan, Rupert, Debolsillo, 2009

Cómo Evaluar las Acciones de Capacitación, Abraham, Pain, Granica, 1993

E-learning: Concepts and Practice, Holmes, Bryn y Gardner John, Sage Publicatios LTD, 2006

Gerardo Soto

He has a degree in Communication Sciences from the Instituto Tecnológico y de Estudios Superiores de Monterrey.

He was sportscaster for Grupo Acir and Televisa from 1998 to 2000.

He has 22 years of experience in the field of training, where he has held various positions such as: Assistant, Instructor, Analyst, and Manager.

He has 16 years of experience as a consultant and has worked for companies such as: Banco Santander, Banamex, Seguros Monterrey New York Life, Banorte, Scotiabank, Roche, HSBC, Cinépolis, Bancomext, Infonavit, Siemens, Comisión Federal de Electricidad, Financiamiento Progresemos, Grupo México and Canon.

He is an expert in topics such as: Strategic Planning, Leadership, Teamwork, Customer Service, Time Management, Communication, Motivation, Change Management and Instructor Training.

He is currently a founding partner and CEO of the consultancy SOLDERH.

www.ingramcontent.com/pod-product-compliance
Lightning Source LLC
Chambersburg PA
CBHW071359210526
45465CB00001B/170